The Old House Book of

Outdoor Living Spaces

Other Titles in the Old House Books Series

The Old House Book of Bedrooms
The Old House Book of Living Rooms and Parlors
The Brand New Old House Catalogue

Forthcoming

The Old House Book of Kitchens and Dining Rooms
The Old House Book of Halls and Stairways

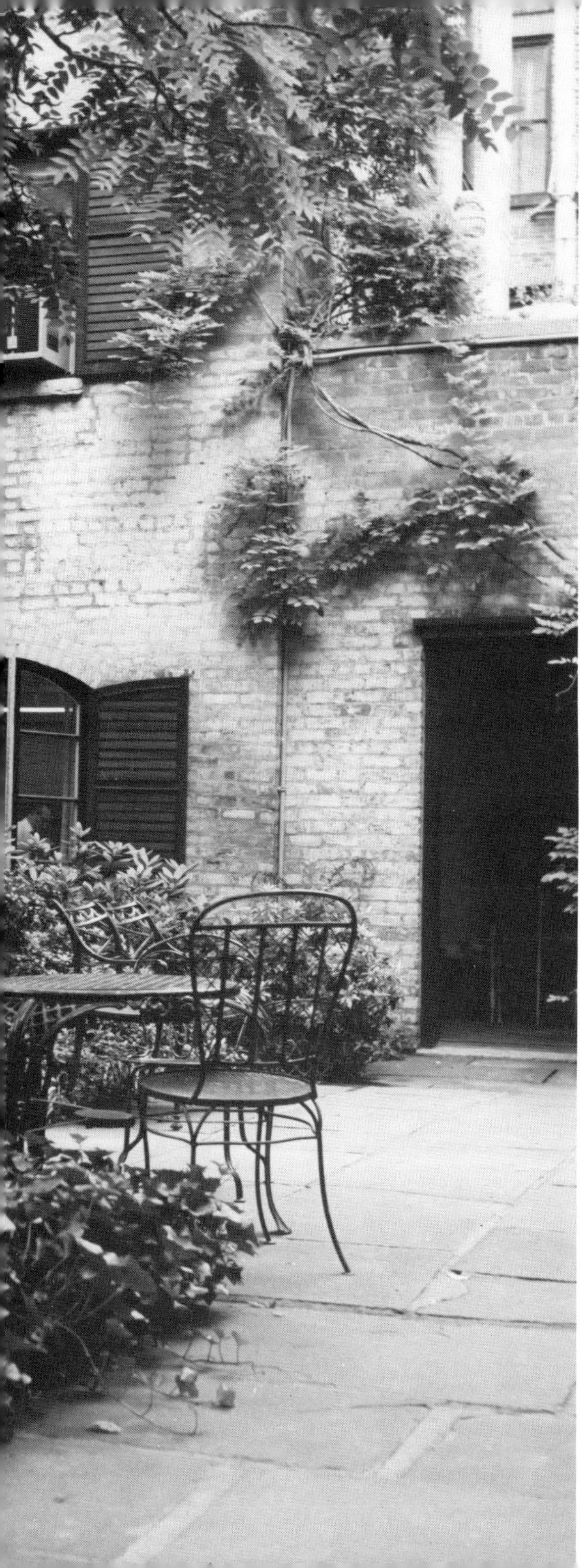

The Old House Book of

Outdoor Living Spaces

Lawrence Grow, General Editor
S. Allen Chambers, Consultant

A Warner Communications Company

A Main Street Press Book

Warner Books, Inc.
75 Rockefeller Plaza
New York, N.Y. 10019

 A Warner Communications Company

Printed in the United States of America

First printing: March 1981

10 9 8 7 6 5 4 3 2 1

Library of Congress Cataloging in Publication Data

The Old House Book of Outdoor Living Spaces.

1. Building—Amateurs' Manuals 2. Dwellings—Remodeling—Amateurs' Manuals. 3. Summer Homes—Amateurs' Manuals. I. Grow, Lawrence. II. Chambers, S. Allen.
TH148.039 690'89 80-20935
ISBN 0-446-51219-2 (hardcover)
ISBN 0-446-97556-7 (pbk. U.S.A.)
ISBN 0-446-97872-8 (Canada)

Contents

Portico, Perkins-Spencer House, Eutaw, Alabama, 1850, T. S. Spence, builder, as photographed in 1934.

Introduction

House and garden are inextricably linked in the popular imagination. The picturesque combinations of house and garden known today and in the past are many — the rose-covered veranda of a Western ranch house; the Federal-style dwelling with its dooryard abloom with lilacs and enclosed by a picket fence; the brick Colonial town house designed to overlook symmetrical rows of flowering plants and borders of boxwood. Even in the close quarters of the city, a contiguous dwelling is often set apart from others by decorative plantings and such small architectural embellishments as balconies and ornamental entryways. It is this outer world of house and garden — of porches, porticos, balconies, terraces, garden sculpture and furniture, summer houses and pergolas, lawn, flowers, trees, and shrubs — which constitutes the subject of *The Old House Book of Outdoor Living Spaces.* The setting of almost any period dwelling calls for as much thoughtful consideration by the home restorer as the interior details.

In 1870 one observer called landscaping "the art of picture making and picture framing, by means of the varied forms of vegetable growth." The writer, Frank J. Scott, ad-

Veranda, Vhay House, Santa Barbara, California, 1825, as photographed in 1934.

dressed himself to the problem of creating romantic effects in a book entitled *The Art of Beautifying Suburban Home Grounds.* A student of A. J. Downing, America's first major landscape architect, Scott understood how important a setting is for any home, new or old. He was conscious, too, of the great advantage possessed by the owner of an old house. "Has the reader ever noticed," he commented, "some remarkably pleasant old home, where little care seemed taken to make it so. . . ." In contrast, Scott observed that the fastidiously landscaped grounds of many recently built Victorian homes failed to convey the same picture of ease and grace. Soft, pleasing effects in the landscape are slowly nurtured and are as much the product of age as they are of planning.

Such grace may be a product of time, but strength and form are not often long-lived in the world of nature. It is theoretically impossible, for example, to restore an 18th-century garden to its original state. Many of the plant specimens used at that time have not survived. Only a handful of these period gardens have been restored to a state *approximating* that known in the past. The majority of the so-called Colonial gardens open to the public are an expression of wish fulfillment, arrangements which please a modern taste for neatness and a profusion of blossom and color.

How might the typical village homestead have appeared in the 18th century? Historian James Marston Fitch has suggested a very different scene than the one encountered today at Colonial Williamsburg or most other museum villages: "For example," he remarks, "most townspeople would have kept a cow, some chickens, and perhaps a pig or two in their backyards. . . .Grass verges between streets and sidewalks would have had a wan-

Before and after remodeling, from the Illustrated Annual Register of Rural Affairs *(1873). The simple Georgian Colonial house was considered "very ordinary and insipid" by the trendsetters of the mid-Victorian period. Every attempt was made to introduce "picturesque" elements—a sweeping veranda, vergeboards, diamond-paned sash—which would render the exterior appearance of the house more appealing and up-to-date.*

The grounds have not been as drastically altered as the house, but the general scene has been improved with a gently curving drive and the addition of outdoor furniture under the tree and on the new veranda. A veranda was often termed an "outdoor living room," and the architect of the remodeled building felt that the space was "equal in value to any room in the house."

dering population of cattle, sheep, swine, and geese. Street trees and fences would have been spotty and unevenly maintained."

We have become so used to closely mowed lawns, immaculately maintained fences and hedgerows, and lavishly tended flower beds that we are often unprepared for surviving evidence of past fashions in landscaping or gardening. The approach to Wye House on Maryland's Eastern Shore, through a private park dotted with trees and knee-high grass, reminds the visitor that a considerable part of the grounds of a Colonial plantation was left virtually untended. Only the grassy areas immediately before and behind the great manor house (illustrated on pp. 40-45) are manicured today with a lawnmower; before the advent of this machine in the mid-1800s, these areas were cut with a scythe several times during the warmer months.

The gardens at Wye, dating back to the mid-17th century, testify to the mix of aesthetic and practical concerns which governed so much of the use of outdoor spaces. Careful archaeological study has confirmed that many of the earliest beds contained a mixture of flowers, vegetables, and herbs. Even the first kitchen garden, located near the original 17th-century manor house, was planted with this combination of varieties. Herbs were most often grown as border plants and rarely separately. "The concept of 'herb gardens,' such as those we often find associated with restored houses," experts Rudy and Joy Favretti have found, "bears little support in the literature" of the Colonial period.

While much plant material may have a limited life, thereby making an exact restoration a very difficult if not impossible proposition, there are important elements in the typical landscape which commonly have retained their character and basic form. Trees are often the most conspicuous example, and a stand of almost any variety is to be prized. Such hardy shrubs as wistaria, spirea, lilac, boxwood, and holly often may have survived years of neglect; so, too, may have beds of peonies. Just as importantly, some semblance of the original plan or landscaping scheme is likely to remain visible. Pruning may be necessary here and there; replanting with modern varieties of old species may be called for in other areas. In any case, as Frank J. Scott wrote in 1870, "it may be safely said that new places rarely afford a skillful planter such opportunities for making quick and beautiful effects at small cost as old places. . . ."

In proceeding to restore or remodel the outdoor living spaces of any old house, knowledge of the progression of styles and forms which have marked the history of home and garden design in North America can be very useful. This story is traced in the following chapters. It is by no means simply a chronicle of the development of plant materials, however essential information about these are to any successful period landscaping scheme. Also important to consider are the various architectural elements of a house—porches, verandas, balconies, galleries, piazzas, arcades, porticos—which help to tie the structure to its surroundings. The first homes of the New World contained few of these embellishments; over time they became increasingly important in home building. Similarly, such unattached structures as the summer house, pergola, pavilion, and bower grew in popularity during the 19th century with an increase in prosperity and leisure time. To furnish both attached and unattached outdoor spaces, special furniture was developed; to embellish a garden, terrace, or

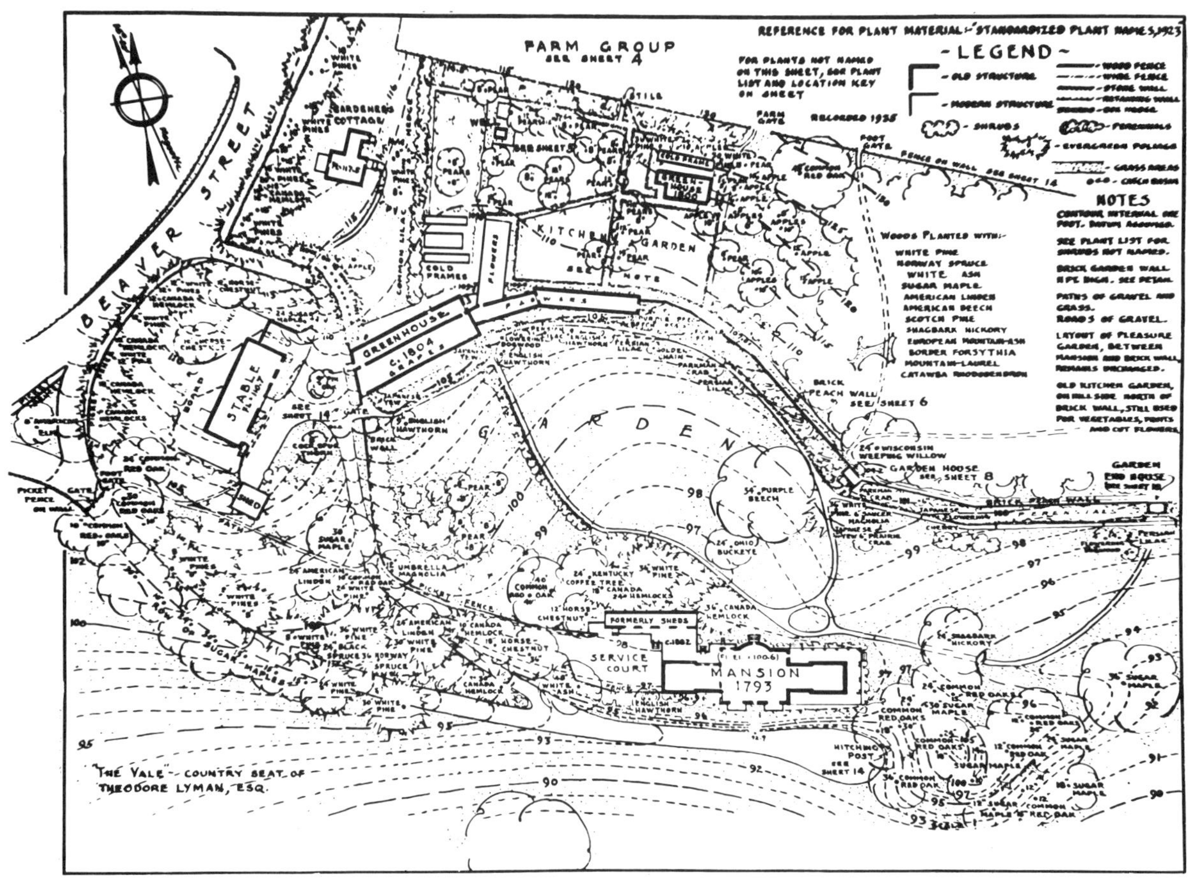

Detail plan of grounds, "The Vale," Waltham, Massachusetts, laid out in 1793. The pleasure garden of the Lyman family estate is among the first in America to have been designed in a "natural" rather than symmetrical manner. The kitchen garden beyond it, however, was laid out in a more formal style. Like other such gardens of the period, it contained a mixture of vegetable, fruit, and flower plantings.

lawn, sculptural forms were introduced.

The historical use of outdoor living spaces and the degree of their elaboration have been determined greatly by the simple matter of climate. In many northern areas houses are not generally provided with such exterior features as verandas and balconies; the buildings appear to be closed in on themselves in self-protection, the openings to the outside kept to a minimum. Only in northern summer resorts is a freer use of exterior space the rule rather than the exception. In contrast, many southern homes in both urban and rural areas present a much more open appearance; the façade of the typical antebellum plantation house with its monu-

Portico, Mount Vernon, Fairfax County, Virginia, added in 1784 by George Washington. Built in 1743, Mount Vernon only gained its familiar form 40 years later. This change, one of many following the Revolution, greatly enhanced the exterior appearance of the main house. Washington followed no known model for the full-length portico. It is considered the first such design executed in North America. Imitation, especially in the South, has never lessened in the following 200 years.

Veranda design from Villas and Cottages *by Calvert Vaux (1857). Vaux, like Frank J. Scott, was a student of A. J. Downing. All agreed that a veranda added much to a home's appearance. "The veranda," Vaux wrote, "is perhaps the most specially American feature in a country house, and nothing can compensate for its absence."*

mental portico is a striking example. Although certain elements of southern architectural expression are borrowed from traditional Mediterranean forms, the basic heritage drawn upon in the South is the same as that known in the North – the northern European culture of the early settlers. Only in subtropical or arid areas of the Deep South or Far West has the southern European influence been strong. It is here that one finds some of North America's most appealing historic homes and gardens. Gracefully designed to take full advantage of the out-of-doors throughout much of the year, they suggest the state of leisure and ease which has been the envy of inhabitants of the snow belt since the early 1900s. Study of the historical record, however, provides much evidence that homes in more temperate regions need not be either barren of pleasant outdoor living spaces or imitative of southern examples. There is considerable variety and experience from the past to be drawn upon.

"The Pagoda," Casa Grande, New Almaden, California, as photographed c. 1885. Many such Victorian summer houses were based on oriental designs or incorporated motifs of this character.

Portico, Robinson-Dilworth House, Huntsville, Alabama, 1840, as photographed in 1935. The Greek Revival style enjoyed enormous popularity in the South for both country and town residences throughout a great deal of the 19th century. The columned portico was the visual keynote of the style and a most graceful manner in which to relate a building to its surroundings.

Playing croquet, Holly House, Warwick, New York, c. 1875. Mid- to late-19th-century homes built in the North are much more likely to feature a veranda than those of an earlier date. Croquet was a popular pastime from the mid-1800s on, and space was often allowed for a properly level court in the side yard. From the appearance of the trees and shrubs, the Second Empire-style residence was only ten years or so old when sketched. The absence of some foundation plantings is unusual in a high-style Victorian house of the period.

1.
From the Inside Out: The Porch, Portico, Veranda and Other Attached Structures

Few homes in early America were built with porches, porticos, verandas, or other attached living spaces. In the North and as far south as Virginia, the primary area of English settlement, little attention was paid to embellishing the exterior of a building with anything more than minor detailing around windows and doors. Neither of these openings to the outside were likely to be very large or numerous. The typical early colonial home was closed in on itself, fortified from the weather and the unknown. In New England the first barns were often extensions of the main house and not separate buildings located across a dooryard. Animals sometimes even shared the home with their masters. Only in the 18th century, and gradually at that, was there a definite move to relate a structure to its natural surroundings.

In the early years of settlement little attention was given to the planting of trees since the natural landscape was well-supplied with virgin stands of oak, pine, maple, and other hardy species. Clearing land for agriculture took precedence over "landscaping," as on any frontier, and only after boundaries were secure, when the land had been enclosed and was producing sufficient crops, did thoughts turn to aesthetic considerations as well as domestic improvements. A few settlers could devote time to the work of beautifying their surroundings at a fairly early date. In the 1660s, for example, the founder of Wye House (see pp. 40-45) was busy laying out a formal garden and building a greenhouse, but such gentlemen of means were the exception. Even in the small coastal cities then taking form, daily life was most likely to be led on a subsistence level. Small outdoor pleasures were enjoyed not at home but on public ground, the bowling green or common.

Settlers were not unaware of architectural aesthetics; they simply had little time for them. But the basic siting of a structure was a far different matter. Sites for homes were chosen, for instance, for both practical *and* picturesque reasons. Unlike the average homebuilder today, the settler could choose between a number of beautiful sites—high, wooded ground that required not ornamental planting but judicious clearing. To place a home in a shaded, well-drained location, and to position it away from the prevailing winds of winter only made good sense. In time, more pleasant use could be made of such fair prospects.

As the colonists improved their economic lot they turned to the mother country for advice in building more imposing homes and in landscaping them. The use of English building manuals and books of designs during the 18th century has been well documented. From the 1720s on, models of a formal, symmetrical regularity—since classified by historians as being Georgian in style—were adopted and adapted in the English colonies. Sash windows, for instance, slowly replaced smaller casement windows in well-balanced rows. A central front entrance was often dressed up with a pedimented doorway design based on a classical order; sometimes, a small open-columned porch or portico was added to the main entrance. By the late 18th century, the neoclassical forms popularized in England by such architects as Robert Adam had become well-established in the colonies.

Above: *A vignette from* Village and Farm Cottages *by Samuel D. Backus, Henry W. Cleaveland, and William Backus (1856). The choice of a proper site for a house and how the main entryway should be fashioned were two important subjects for the writers of 19th-century building manuals.*

Below: *Batchelor's Hope, Chaptico vicinity, St. Mary's County, Maryland, before 1750. The formal qualities of the Georgian Colonial style are strikingly evident in this perfectly balanced 18th-century plantation house. The classical wood portico is enclosed by the central block in the form of an entryway.*

As the English Colonial styles in America were evolving, so, too, were the Spanish Colonial as well as the French. Both rural and urban homes built in areas settled by the two Latin peoples in the 17th and 18th centuries may display such traditional architectural features as balconies and galleries, arcades or colonnades, and inner courtyards or patios. It was only natural that a more open style of domestic architecture would take root in these warmer sections of the country. In the French areas of the Mississippi Valley, some of the earliest buildings were designed with a colonnade running around all four sides; in the Southeast—from Charleston to New Orleans—wrought-iron balconies and galleries embellish the façades of some of the most historic dwellings. In the Southwest and in the Far West, Indian building methods and Spanish forms were combined in the medium of adobe to create one of the most pleasing and natural of Colonial-period styles. The early clay or adobe house, however, did not display much exterior elaboration. These rural homes, like those of the 17th-century English settlements in the East, were built at first as protective fortresses with few exterior openings. It is the inner courtyard, the medieval *placita* or patio, which most distinguishes the early Spanish Colonial dwelling from that of the English. Not until the 19th century were casement windows introduced and such attachments as porches and verandas made to the outer walls.

The addition of porches or porticos to English Colonial dwellings in the late 1700s signalled the beginning of an elaboration of the exterior and was an expression of a desire to include impressive and pleasant outdoor living spaces. This was especially true in the Middle Atlantic and Southern states. Wye House on Maryland's Eastern Shore, for example, was built first in the 1780s without a front portico, but within several years a Palladian-style structure with benches for seating at each side was added to the main entrance. It was in the 1780s, too, that George Washington drastically remodeled

Above: *Cantilevered porch, San Juan, Puerto Rico, 19th century. Time and neglect have not erased the beauty of the ornamental ironwork used structurally to form graceful balconies and porches in areas first colonized by the Spanish.*

Below: *Ralph M. Munroe House (The Barnacles), Coconut Grove, Miami, Florida, as photographed before* (left) *and after 1908* (right). *Although built in the late 1800s, this home is strikingly similar in design to those known in the Mississippi Valley more than 100 years earlier. The original one-story house with a veranda wrapping around three sides resembles the square hip-roofed structures erected by the French is Kaskaskia, Illinois, and Ste. Genevieve, Missouri. As remodeled with the addition of a second story (the first having been raised), the effect is one of a Victorian antebellum house kin to those of Mississippi and Louisiana. The historical parallels may be explained in terms of building traditions and of climate. In a hot and humid region, the need for ventilation and shade suggested such an architectural treatment.*

Left: *Umbria, near Sawyerville, Alabama, early 19th century, as photographed in 1934. The neoclassic elegance of this stuccoed brick plantation home is established not only by the formal entryway with fan- and sidelights or the heavy cornice and entablature, but by the full-width portico and its Ionic columns.*

Below (left and right): *Tyson House, Lowndesboro, Alabama, mid-19th century, as photographed in 1934. A gallery was often placed over the front entrance of an antebellum or southern Greek Revival home. It is an aesthetically pleasing and practical addition to a two-story portico. With railings fashioned in cast iron, the gallery has a graceful, airy appearance.*

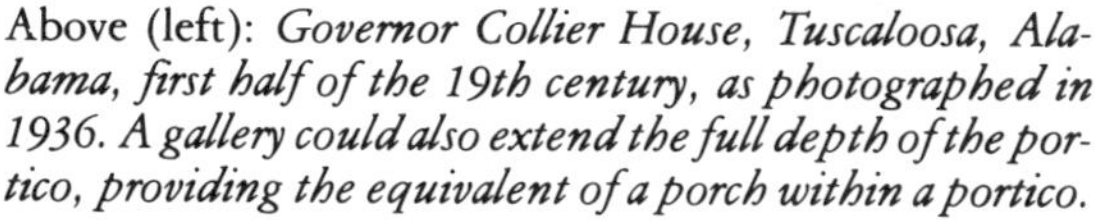

Above (left): *Governor Collier House, Tuscaloosa, Alabama, first half of the 19th century, as photographed in 1936. A gallery could also extend the full depth of the portico, providing the equivalent of a porch within a portico.*

Above (right): *Montgomery Place, Barrytown, Red Hook, New York, 1802; additions made in the 1840s and 1860s by Alexander J. Davis, architect. A veranda might be suitable for a modest dwelling, but something more grand was called for up the Hudson in the mid-19th century. By the 1840s the original two-story Federal home of the Livingston family was a dignified, but old-fashioned dwelling. Davis was commissioned to make alterations, and the addition of the semi-circular portico seen here nearly ruined the family and the house. Mrs. Clara Livingston Barton, then the owner, recorded her initial distress over the design based on the Temple of Vesta in Tivoli:*

> The columns are up & the entablature is progressing. The whole thing per se is beautiful—but alas! it squashes down the whole house, & as one of the ancients said: "Who tied my son to that sword"! so I exclaim Who has clapped my old house to the Temple of Vesta! The addition to the top of the house becomes a necessity & is the only thing to save us from a monstrous incongruity . . . anything rather than this beautiful, overwhelming Portico should look so out of proportion with the main house . . . You wicked man, with your Temple of Vesta to lead me to all this ruinous extravagance; which I cannot now avoid without being ridiculous.

As Mrs. Barton noted, the roof of the original house had to be raised a half floor. But, with 20th-century hindsight, the move was a small price to pay. Davis's design was well in advance of his time; not until the Beaux Arts period later in the century was such a classical addition at all common for a stately home.

Middle: *Orange Grove (Silcox House), Anderson, South Carolina, 19th century, as photographed in 1960. Four different stages were involved in the building of this home, the last of which included the addition of the second-story portico and the immense veranda.*

Above: *Grand Hotel, Mackinac Island, Michigan, 1887. The Grand is not singular as a resort hotel, but it is one of the largest of such colonnaded buildings erected in summer watering spots from coast to coast during the 1800s. No proper Victorian retreat was without some architectural provision for outdoor living.*

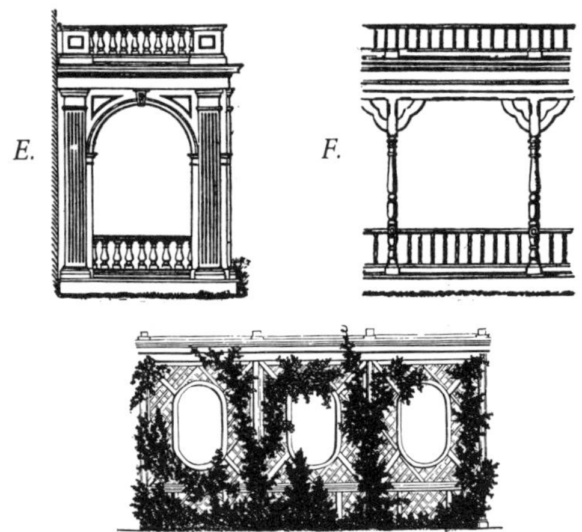

Designs for verandas varied greatly according to the style of the dwelling. Calvert Vaux in Villas and Cottages *(1857) suggested several variations, including "E," appropriate for an Italianate or Tuscan villa, and "F," with bracketed and turned columns. Verandas could also be partially enclosed, latticework being commonly used.*

Mount Vernon, raising the roof to provide a second story and a columned portico running the full width of the house. In the North additions such as these were much less common, and the popular Federal style of the 1780s through the early 1800s called for a more chaste pilastered façade which did not project onto the grounds. By the 1830s, nevertheless, a new and romantic style of building—the Greek Revival—had caught the fancy of the public in all areas of the country. Although not every house in this style featured a classical portico, many were near replicas of ancient temples. The style would persist in popularity throughout the century south of the Mason-Dixon line. In the North, however, the tastemakers of the 1840s were touting the aesthetic superiority of the Gothic Revival and Italianate styles.

The series of architectural revivals commencing with the Gothic brought with it ever increasing attention to the exterior decoration of a house and provision for picturesque outdoor areas. These took several forms, but the most common was the veranda. A term of either Hindi or Spanish derivation, a veranda (or verandah) differs from a porch in that it is most often a more fanciful, decorative structure. Rather than occupying one corner of a house, a veranda often extends the full length of the front, and may even wrap around one or two sides. Like a porch, a veranda may rise two or even three stories, but it is often overladen with decorative cast-ironwork or gingerbread. Columns carry the weight of the roof, and between these supports, most typically, are railings, balusters, and brackets. Today the spaces between these elements are left open or screened; in the 19th century they were sometimes filled with latticework or trellises. No proper veranda, it would seem from the pictorial record, was without a climbing plant of some sort—wistaria, rose, trumpet vine, grape vine, or other ornamental climbers.

In contrast to the 18th-century entryway porch or portico designed primarily for greeting guests, the veranda provided ample space for everyday outdoor living. It was furnished with a suitable set of furniture, rockers and swings being popular for many years. As architect Lewis Allen wrote in 1851, "many southern people almost live under the shade of their verandas. It is a delightful place to take their meals, to receive their visitors and friends; and the veranda gives to a dwelling the very expression of hospitality so far as any one feature of a dwelling can do it."

Most verandas were constructed of wood, with turned or square posts, railings, spindles, or balusters. As the 19th century progressed, the form of these elements became more and more fanciful. The moongate archway seen in the veranda of many Queen Anne houses is one such imaginative ornamental form. Spandrels, brackets, corbels, drops—fancy fretwork of all sorts was introduced in the spaces between the columns to enhance the picturesque quality of the structure. Similar in ornamentation were the cast-iron verandas which became especially popular in southern coastal cities during the mid-19th century. Many of the delicate designs seen in the South were based on patterns worked by hand in wrought iron at considerable cost in earlier years. Cast iron was a much less expensive

Right: *Moffitt House, Montgomery, Alabama, 19th century, as photographed in 1935. Latticework panels give this veranda an air of privacy and effectively screen the direct sunlight while still providing ventilation.*

Below (left): *The mid- to late-Victorian porch or veranda was often ornately decorated with a variety of machine-turned and cut wooden forms—brackets, spindles, corbels, pendants, dentils, and moldings. The porch seen here is from a Savannah, Georgia, home but could have been assembled from available millwork in almost any area of the country in the second half of the 19th century.*

Below (right): *Two-tier porches and verandas are found most often in the South, their utility being more obvious in this region than in the North. The handsome example shown here is from Savannah, and appears to be attached to the rear of the house.*

Robinson-Jordan House, New Orleans, Louisiana, 1865, James Gallier, Jr., architect. Both wood and cast-iron two-tier verandas were included in the plans for this Garden District mansion. The use of cast iron in such a delicate and romantic manner greatly pleased the Victorians and remains a delight today.

medium, and highly imaginative forms—even whole verandas—were mass produced in an artistic manner in both the North and the South. Ready-to-assemble elements were sometimes shipped thousands of miles from the point of manufacture.

In the towns and cities of the West the preferred mode of home building in the second half of the 19th century mirrored that in more settled areas of the country. Some of the most elaborately contrived Victorian-period façades—in the Queen Anne or Eastlake styles—are still to be found in those areas of the West where lumber was most plentiful and cheap. The building manuals of the 1870s and '80s are full of designs which make of the façade a complex interplay of form and function. A veranda, a piazza, an entryway porch with balcony, a two-story balcony—each supplied a visual and spatial opening to the outdoors. This was a time, too, when foundation plantings were becoming popular, when lawnmowers became available to keep grass closely cropped, when outdoor games

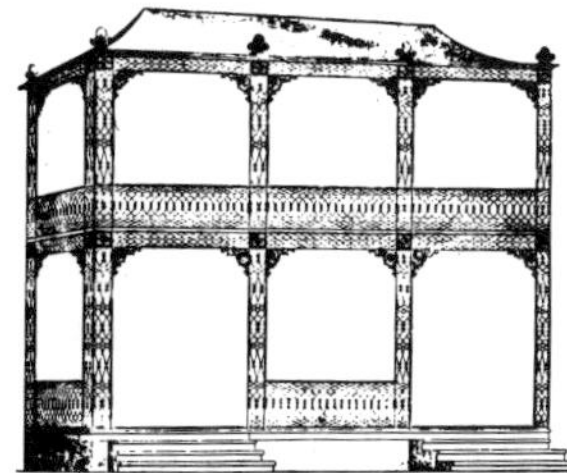

Left: *Two composite wrought- and cast-iron veranda designs from the New York Wire Railing Co. catalogue, 1857. This New York firm was one of the most prominent in the country. "In one of these delightful shelters," the copywriter extolled, "there is a sense of enjoyment to be found that can be had nowhere else. . . .Through them comes the view of pleasant twilights, and the evening breezes blow sweetly among the climbing plants that cover them."*

Below: *Cast-iron and composite wire found use as well in entrance steps, and in porch and veranda railings. At the entrance to the formal Hampton-Preston mansion in Columbia, South Carolina, cast-iron elements provide a light and graceful note to what is—overall—a massive design.*

such as croquet, badminton, and lawn tennis became fashionable. The average town or city dweller—in whatever part of the country—had more money to spend and more leisure time in which to enjoy it out of doors.

The exterior decoration and additions made to the typical rural home in the Victorian period remained much simpler. The veranda of the one or one-and-a-half story country house stretched across the width of the front, the space between the columns often being left open. Usually built at ground level and not raised on a high foundation, there was no need for fancy railings or balusters to enclose the structure. These homes are not far in character from the simple cottages sketched by A. J. Downing and other architectural critics and builders of the

Right: *Side porch and balcony, Olana, Church Hill, New York, 1874, Frederic Church, designer, Calvert Vaux, architect. The architectural fantasy that is Olana must have taken form in artist Church's imagination for many years. Tucked away at the corners and multitude of angles are numerous projections—porches and balconies—which are imaginative observation posts on the surrounding Hudson Valley countryside. Few late-Victorian houses are as imaginative or eclectic in design as Church's creation, but many lavishly indulge the desire for picturesque and varied external forms and decoration.*

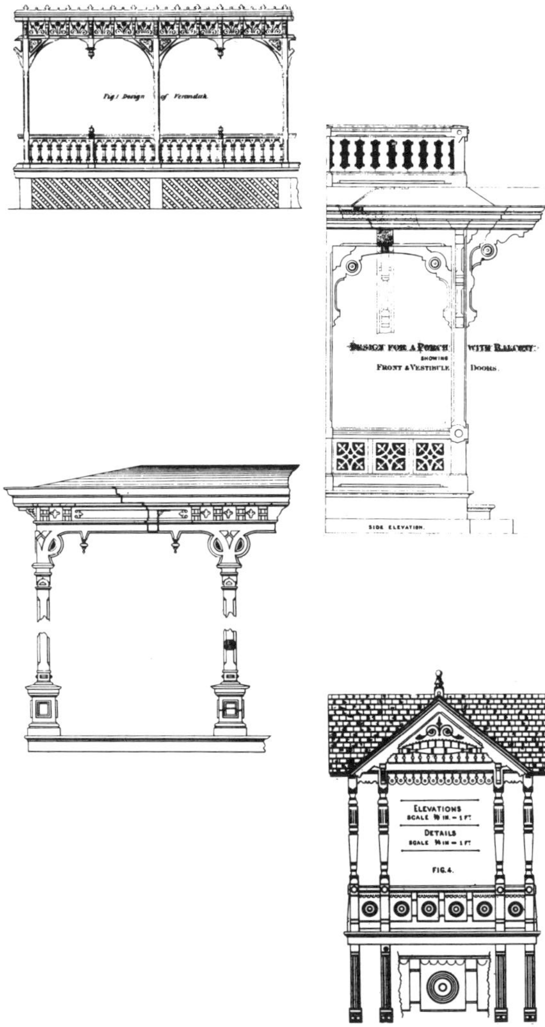

Four designs from William Comstock's Modern Architectural Designs and Details *(1881) illustrate the variety of forms used in the high-style Queen Anne house in the last decades of the 1800s. First is the veranda; second, a porch with balcony; third, a piazza or open side porch; and last, a balcony supported on columns.*

mid-century. For them an enclosed or an "arbor-veranda" (with open rafters), and a bay window were considered sufficient exterior features to convey pride in home and to provide domestic comfort. Few others were needed when the outdoors was everywhere around and leisure time was extremely limited. Only country gentlemen possessed the means to keep up with the changing fashions dictated during the Victorian period by their suburban and urban brethren.

By the early 20th century there was a turning away from the highly ornamental forms and motifs of the high Victorian era by this fashionable class. The "revival" spirit of the 1800s was not dead, however, and manifested itself in a new appreciation for the Colonial in both its English and Spanish forms. Perhaps more colonnaded antebellum houses were built throughout the country during the years 1920 to 1940 than had been erected in the first half of the 19th century in all of the South. Georgian Colonial Revival homes were popular, too, most of them featuring a simple columned entryway and two side porches—"sun porches" or "piazzas." Porches for summertime sleeping on the second floor were a must in many early 20th-century homes. Spanish Colonial Revival houses boasting wrought-iron balconies and arched entryways with iron gates sprang up in the most un-Hispanic of places—Milwaukee, Richmond, Indianapolis. Regional differences and traditions were blurred, and so, too, were climatic distinctions. Indoor-outdoor garden or "Florida" rooms could be found in upper-class homes across the country; supplied with French doors that opened onto a terrace or sun porch, the room was a less stuffy successor to the Victorian conservatory.

Gradually a more original style of domestic architecture took form in sophisticated circles across the country. The wood-framed homes of Greene and Greene in California and those of Frank Lloyd Wright and his contemporaries in the Midwest share in common a massive structural horizontality, with porches or decks wrapping around the core of the buildings in a streamlined fashion. Such designs provided handsome settings for carefully composed foundation plantings. The landscaping of the grounds emphasized the broad sweep of the structures. Perhaps as never before, the American home was integrated with its natural surroundings.

Most Americans in the first several decades of the 20th century—as previously—lived in far simpler homes. Among those that were "new" in the opening years of the present century, a majority can be defined as "bungalow." Borrowed from India, the word "bungalow" entered the American building vocabulary in the late 19th century and is a style which first flourished in such fast-growing areas of the country as California. A bungalow is usually a narrow one or one-and-a-half story house with bedrooms at the rear, dining room and kitchen in the center, and a living room and entry hall at the front. The typical bungalow has an open front porch which is either cut out from the main structure or attached to it; some feature an enclosed sun porch. The bungalow was for the working class what the cottage was in the early to mid-19th century—a low-price, compact residence. It contained many of the elements of a finer home, but on a reduced scale. In areas of the country where the weather stays relatively mild during much of the year—the mid- and deep South and West Coast—this form of building was naturally chosen. The bungalow was the last form of vernacular domestic architecture to feature a full porch. In recent years, however, some of the

Nick Prevost House, Anderson, South Carolina, 1876-77. From superficial appearances, the Prevost House would seem to have been built much earlier in the century. The neoclassical spirit is so strong in the shapes and elements of the arcaded porch and in the balustrade of the roof that one is tempted to assign the design to the late 18th century. Nick Prevost, however, modeled his house after one shown at the 1876 Philadelphia Centennial Exposition. Low-lying and generously endowed with outdoor spaces, it is a fitting design for a Southern home. The use of Renaissance-inspired arches, inverted balusters, and decorative pediments with acorns suggests that some architects were beginning to tire of the Victorian Gothic and were returning to neoclassical or Colonial designs for inspiration.

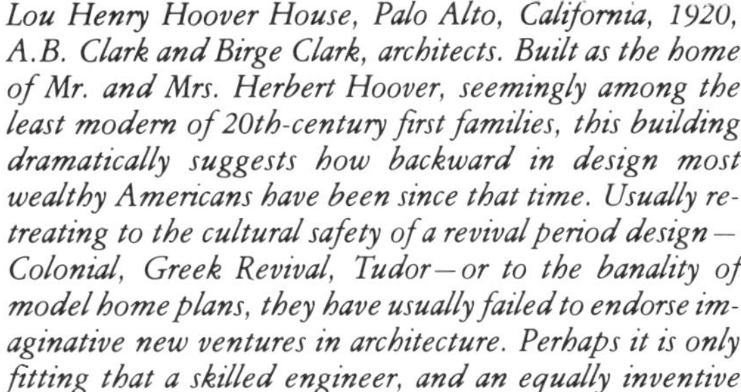

Lou Henry Hoover House, Palo Alto, California, 1920, A.B. Clark and Birge Clark, architects. Built as the home of Mr. and Mrs. Herbert Hoover, seemingly among the least modern of 20th-century first families, this building dramatically suggests how backward in design most wealthy Americans have been since that time. Usually retreating to the cultural safety of a revival period design—Colonial, Greek Revival, Tudor—or to the banality of model home plans, they have usually failed to endorse imaginative new ventures in architecture. Perhaps it is only fitting that a skilled engineer, and an equally inventive wife, should have desired a house which brought together, in Hoover's words, his wife's "own blend of fine living and the new spirit of native western architecture." The terrace areas are vast and functional, practical use having been made of the various roof levels. The enjoyment of the outdoors—a prerequisite of modern California living—is well provided for. A pergola is perched on the highest level; an outdoor fireplace was installed at one end of the second-floor terrace. Since 1944 the house has been the residence of Stanford University's presidents.

houses have been remodeled; the porch spaces have been filled in with permanent windows or jalousies, thereby creating another "indoor" room but eliminating the open, hospitable appearance once thought so desirable. Open front porches, of course, were more pleasant places before streets became mere raceways from one part of town to another, and the enclosed porch became the most logical solution to the bungalow's inherent problem—a shortage of space.

By the mid-20th century the average home had been "climatized" in a way that the fresh-air enthusiasts of the late 1800s could never imagine. By the 1960s, it was often no longer necessary to go out of doors to "cool off" or to enjoy a breeze. The utility of a veranda, porch, or portico was unquestioned at a time when it was not possible to adjust the temperature with a flick of a switch. While houses may never again be as open to the outside as they were in the late 19th century, there is today an unmistakable return to those architectural forms which provided so much delight in the past. The cost of cooling a house has so increased that the porch and the deck are seen as practical and as attractive features. Today's well-designed contemporary home makes use of varied levels and structural forms to keep the dwelling as naturally cool in summer and as warm in winter as possible. Such practicality, the historical record shows, can bring with it imaginative results.

2.
Leisurely Open Spaces: The Patio, Terrace, and Courtyard

Until the late 19th century, few Americans would have recognized a patio or courtyard even if they had had an opportunity to travel far beyond the confines of their towns and villages. The small outposts of Spanish and French culture in the South and the West, where such outdoor spaces could be found, were far removed from the mainstream of Anglo-American life. To build a home with such an outdoor space as a patio, as is done today throughout North America, would have made no sense to the average citizen who lived in a distinct four-season climate. A terrace was a better-known feature of the domestic landscape, although in the 18th and 19th centuries this space was more likely to be a grassy embankment or mount rather than the paved area designated a terrace in recent years.

The patio and courtyard are those outdoor spaces which lie closest to the house. They are traditionally formed by the walls of a dwelling, creating what is an inner-outer living area reached easily from several rooms of the house. Neither a patio nor a courtyard need be enclosed on all four sides; three or even two sides will suffice. The patio, however, should not be confused, as it often is today, with a terrace lying alongside one wall of the house.

During the Colonial period there were scattered attempts to affect the landscaping features of the English pleasure garden or park which may have included terraced spaces. The Lloyds of Wye House (see pp. 40-45) and other members of the landed gentry met with some success in this respect, terracing land to produce romantic bowers, laying out a smooth bowling green from the main house to a pavilion or greenhouse. Until late in the eighteenth century, however, these attempts were circumscribed by a lack of trained experts in the art of landscaping.

After the Revolution members of the upper class vied to improve the grounds of their city and country homes. The story of the development of "The Vale," the Lyman family estate in Waltham, Massachusetts, and Thomas Jefferson's "Monticello" is told in chapter 4. The problems of moving earth, of creating dramatic effects in the landscape, of securing hardy and appropriate specimen plants, and of maintaining lavish grounds were enormous, even in those areas of the early Republic where slave labor was available. There was in rural areas, however, an abundance of naturally beautiful sites for development. And in such cities as Philadelphia, Charleston, New York,

Left: *Rear patio, Calle de la Cruz, San Juan, Puerto Rico. If it were not for the appurtenances of 20th-century life visible here, time might have stood still for at least 200 years. Even the simplest dwelling in a crowded section of an early Spanish settlement was often built with a partially enclosed patio that could be used by day to perform domestic tasks and, when work was laid aside in the evening, for relaxation.*

Below: *Courtyard, 701 Bourbon Street, New Orleans, Louisiana. No contemporary designer could hope to recreate the relaxed and colorful setting of this stone-paved courtyard in the French quarter. The second-story balconies provide a natural perch for potted plants and hanging baskets and, of course, the posts for the common clothesline.*

and Boston there was still sufficient room to lay out spacious gardens and other outdoor amenities such as brick walks, garden seats, sundials, classical urns, and other sculptured objects. Neither urban nor rural homes, however, were designed around patios or courtyards of the traditional sort known in Europe.

In the South and West settlers from Latin countries followed many of the Old World building customs with which they were familiar, adapting these over time to local climatic and social conditions. In many areas of France and Spain the homes of the merchant class as well as of the aristocracy had been traditionally protected from the elements and the criminally-inclined by high walls broken only by very small windows and by a carriageway leading to a rear courtyard or patio. In New Orleans and other settled areas of the Louisiana Territory both the Spanish and the French erected homes built around center courtyards, space as useful for storing provisions as it was for growing herbs, vegetables, and flowers. The dwellings of the merchants of the French communities were often multipurpose, the ground floor providing space for a shop, and the second floor, living quarters. The small windows at ground level in the Old

Patio, Johnson-Taylor Ranch House, San Diego, California, built prior to 1883, as photographed c. 1890. The astonishingly contemporary-looking adobe house stood at the center of an important cattle-raising and fruit-growing rancho. *It is representative of the type of sprawling one-story structure built throughout the Southwest. A veranda or arcade protects the house from the sun and lines three sides of the luxuriant patio garden.*

World were replaced in the New with a series of French doors permitting public entry, and which were well-secured by shutters at night. The buildings along Front Street in Natchitoches, Louisiana (see pp. 49-50), are typical of the homes built by French merchants and traders in the late 18th and early 19th centuries.

In the more distant rural areas settled by the French, the first homes were square hip-roofed buildings with porches wrapping around three or four sides. There was rarely provision for a courtyard or patio. By the mid-19th century, the new homes of prosperous French planters resembled the Greek Revival antebellum temples of other South-

McAneeny-Howerdd House (Casa Della Porta), Palm Beach, Florida, c. 1928, Maurice Fatio, architect. William Joseph McAneeny was the president of the Hudson Motor Car Co., and Fatio, a society architect from New York. Together they created a home worthy of a Portuguese or Spanish grandee. Left: *View from north logia. The central patio is enclosed on three sides by arcaded loggias of five bays; the fourth side serves as a service wing.* Above (left): *East loggia. The barrel-vaulted ceiling is hung with wrought-iron lanterns; the floor is composed of unglazed hexagonal clay tiles crisscrossed with rectangular tiles and coral rock pavers.* Above: *Patio. Not even Mrs. Harvey Firestone, who in the 1930s helped to popularize the semi-classical tune "In a Monastery Garden," could have meditated in a more splendid private sanctuary. The patio base is formed of broken coral rock, and at its center four griffons uphold the monumental fountain.*

eastern rural landowners. The dwellings of the less prosperous were what might be termed bungalows today, one- or one-and-a-half story rectangles with perhaps a porch or veranda extending the full width of the front, as seen in the Tante Huppé House (p. 57). At the rear, as in many town houses, there was often a full second-story balcony; the area below this was laid out as a covered and spacious terrace.

The classic Spanish adobe hacienda or southwestern ranch is one source of the modern patio or courtyard. The center courtyard form gradually took shape in the 17th and 18th centuries when several linked units were added to a center block in the form of an "L" or inverted "U"; a wall may

Chester C. Bolton House (Casa Apava), Palm Beach, Florida, main house, c. 1918-19; addition, 1929. Frances Bolton, a United States representative from Ohio during the 1940s and '50s, and her husband, a United States senator in the '30s, had their house built after their marriage. Left: *View from south. The main house was designed by James A. Garfield, son of the President, and the addition, including the library seen at right, was designed by Prentice Sanger. The main house is considerably more eclectic in style than the McAneeny dwelling; porches and terraces comprise the outdoor living spaces.* Below: *North end of library. Sanger endowed his addition with detailing of the Spanish Renaissance. A patio decorated with yellow and blue tiles, a masonry table and bench, and a hexagonal basin and fountain adjoin the library and main house; beyond the traditional patio lies a modern swimming pool and terrace.*

have extended across the last remaining side or sides. In areas where the threat of Indian attack remained real until the end of the 19th century, this type of building, very much like a stockade, was of obvious practical use. The courtyard or *placita* was also a place where flowers could be grown, and—in times of relaxation—where meals could be taken. The original building of the Los Poblanas ranch north of Albuquerque (see pp. 46-48) is known to have been built in the inverted "U" form, the center open space comprising the patio or courtyard, as it does today. This type of building, as well as the mission complexes of the Franciscan fathers, served as models for the great flowering of Spanish Colonial Revival and "Mediterranean" architecture of the late 19th and early 20th centuries. The more modest country homes of the West and the Southwest—perhaps only a single low-lying unit with a protective porch or veranda, but without ells or wings—was to give birth to the bastardized ranch house of the 20th century, with its "patio" that is rarely enclosed or laid out in a manner that relates it to the house.

By the late 19th century many of the areas of the South first settled by the French and Spanish were receiving a steady stream of Northern vacationers. The east coast of Florida was particularly favored. New homes built there as winter residences from the 1890s through the 1930s can best be described as "Mediterranean" in style. They make lavish and imaginative use of such traditional spaces as the courtyard or patio and the terrace. Some of the elaborate mansions of Palm Beach County, for example, display a mixed parentage of the English Tudor Revival and Spanish Colonial; others combine features of the Spanish Romanesque with the lighter forms of the Gothic. Almost all of the homes have steeply pitched roofs of red Cuban tile, and the walls are most often stuccoed. The basic

Cooke-Spaulding House, Honolulu, Hawaii, 1926, Goodhue Associates, architects; additions in the mid-1930s by Harry Brent and, in 1954, under the supervision of Kenneth F. Brown. This striking wood and textured masonry residence was designed to express a harmonious blend of Eastern and Western architectural and landscaping traditions. Opposite page (above): *The original house is set amid grounds which emphasize in formal plantings and raised beds the strong geometric lines of the building.* Opposite page (below): *At the rear, two arcaded porches join to form a handsome patio.* Below: *The most recent addition to the house adjoins a pool area which displays a sensitive understanding of contemporary design and its relation to older architectural form.*

house plan provides for all the major ground floor rooms to be disposed around a central courtyard. This area was not—as it so often is today—devoted to a swimming pool, but to a formal garden as romantic as those to be found in Seville or Toledo. In "Mediterranean" houses that have survived architecturally intact, a fountain usually rests at the center of the space, and around it are arranged beds of flowers and shrubs. The concept of a monastery garden—a cool, quiet, protected space in which to relax—was an immensely popular one in the early 1900s. The swimming pool, therefore, is most likely to be located in a separate area of the grounds and is provided with its own terrace surround.

The desire to enjoy the perquisites of the vacationing rich, to live year round in what has been popularly considered a relaxed manner, has strongly affected the development of 20th-century architecture throughout North America. Modern methods of heating and cooling a house have made possible greater flexibility in design and construction. Modest versions of the grand "Mediterranean" houses of Florida and the Spanish Colonial Revival villas of the Far West were built in all areas of North America during the 1920s and '30s. Some of these designs are rather handsome adaptations, and although few of the houses provide for a central courtyard, they do incorporate a patio, enclosed by two or three walls, which can be reached from graceful arcades or loggias. These outdoor spaces are clearly related to the overall composition of the structures and are not tacked on to the back of the house as became the unhappy custom in the 1950s with the development of the modern "terrace," a sort-of concrete or bricked-in back yard.

3.
A Portfolio of Period Houses and Gardens

The gardens of historic houses are among the most popular tourist attractions in North America. The pleasure of visiting a colorful, well-tended display of floral beauty is undeniable. At a time when many of the public gardens of our large cities are allowed to deteriorate further each year, every square foot of private green space is appreciated when it is treated with care. Even if the plants displayed are not "old" varieties, there often is something about their arrangement which suggests the graceful, comforting fashions of the past. So much popular attention, however, is often devoted to period gardens that little thought is given to other concerns equally interesting—to the design of an attractive porch or portico, for example, or to how a patio or terrace can be integrated with the rest of the property. Examples of the ways in which these and similar problems have been attacked and successfully resolved over the years are presented in the following pages.

Only a few of the properties illustrated have been officially declared "historic," and none are open to the public on any regular basis. Each is a private place, refreshingly free of showy effects designed to impress a paying visitor. Each is a home that is lived in today, and the wide variety of outdoor living spaces shown—from porches to patios to allées of flowers and shrubs—are representative of those to be found in various areas of North America. More than half are from the South or Southwest, those regions in which outdoor living can be appreciated throughout the changing seasons. A majority of the grounds are laid out in an English manner; several owe their form to Spanish or French precedents. Although the properties date from the mid-17th century to the 1920s, their interest to us today derives from timeless qualities of imaginative design worthy of any historical period.

America's First Classical Revival House

Whitehall, near Annapolis, Maryland, a National Historical Landmark and private residence, is America's first Classical Revival house. Built as a summer pleasure palace in 1764-65 by Horatio Sharpe (1718-90), royal governor of Maryland, it was sited and designed to beautify and dignify a broad sweep of land leading to Chesapeake Bay.

The rear façade of what became in time a monumental Georgian Colonial mansion faces away from the Bay and toward pastures and woods. Fortifications were needed in the 18th century to protect the residents from marauders; the embankment, with a cannon set at each of four corners, encloses a broad courtyard.

Colonial America possessed little of the stately rural grandeur of Georgian England. Whitehall was and is an architectural anomaly. Governor Sharpe originally conceived of only the central temple, a grand pavilion with withdrawing rooms at each side, that would be suitable for entertaining. Gradually during the late 1760s, extensions took form at each side of the main structure, of which four remain today. These were intended to provide the space required for routine domestic life. Addition of these rooms, however, did not diminish the dramatic effect of positioning a Corinthian-columned, Palladian-style temple at the very summit of a gradually sloping rise. The wide portico, built nearly twenty years before America's most famous at Mount Vernon, projects onto the greensward, a formal but welcoming architectural statement unique for its time and place.

Until the late 18th century, most stately American homes presented a handsome but relatively plain façade not unlike that seen on the back side of Whitehall. If economics did not dictate a fortress-like appearance, the uncertain conditions of frontier living did. Little time and money could be devoted to the genteel follies of the landed gentry. Even Whitehall could not remain a place of seasonal hospitality for long. Governor Sharpe retired there in 1769 but four years later, on a trip to England, he elected to stay abroad. The home was left to his private secretary.

Guests at the Governor's summer retreat arrived from Annapolis by boat and, upon reaching the dock, proceeded by carriage up the 400-foot-long green allée to the neoclassical pavilion.

Left: *A well house to one side of the front of Whitehall was added in this century. Based on designs of a preexisting structure, it testifies to the aesthetic attention lavished upon even the most simple and functional of outbuildings which might adorn a well-tended domestic landscape.*

Below: *Outdoor swimming pools were not known in the 18th century, and their placement today on the grounds of historic homes is fraught with peril. The present owners of Whitehall chose a shady mound off one end of the front grounds and created an elliptical reflecting pool which, rather than interrupting the flow of the landscape, makes the scene even more inviting.*

A New 18th-Century Garden

To lay out a new 18th-century-style garden today is practically unheard of. To execute successfully such a project is nearly unprecedented. Flowers, vegetables, herbs, and fruits are mixed together in this recently completed private suburban Philadelphia garden. The site is a sloping one, and the landscape architect, Charles Gale & Son, chose to work on two levels, the larger of the two visible below being devoted primarily to flowering plants, shrubs, and ornamental trees. Boxwood defines the symmetrical walks and the elliptical beds. The lower area contains grape vines, espaliered apple trees, and rectangular beds containing both flowers and vegetables. Some varieties used in the 18th century are found in both areas, each specimen being carefully chosen for color, form, and seasonal hardiness.

The garden is enclosed by a picket fence, and at one corner by a fieldstone retaining wall. A sundial on the upper level is positioned at the exact axis of two walks as it would have been in the past.

The landscape architect's perspective drawing emphasizes the regularity of form popular until the advent of a more natural or romantic style in the early 1800s.

A garden house, designed after a Colonial Williamsburg smokehouse, provides space for the drying of herbs and for potting. Attached to one side are two clay birdhouses original to the period.

Several varieties of apples were to be found in many Colonial homesteads, this fruit providing not only food but drink as well. In more formal settings, dwarf varieties were espaliered in the French fashion, their appearance being valued as much as their use.

Real-life peacocks were often found in English pleasure gardens but were rarely seen in 18th-century America. A Colonial garden, however, can be a rather dull place if some poetic license is not taken with its appointments. More true to history are beds at each side in which late-blooming day lilies flourish between two rows of now dormant asparagus plants.

A Colonial Plantation

Wye House has stood virtually undisturbed for nearly 200 years. Situated on a plantation of seemingly endless acreage on Maryland's Eastern Shore, the property has remained in the hands of one family since the mid-17th century. "The charm of the great house," as one historian has written, "is its naturalness and its authenticity . . . " The fortunate visitor can also discover much that is genuinely charming and instructive in the outbuildings behind the mansion, in the formal garden superimposed in the 1780s over one laid out in the 1600s, in the surviving dependency of the original Wye House of c. 1660, and in the orangerie, a greenhouse first built in the 17th century and enlarged a century later.

Only the Wye House sundial remains of several decorative and utilitarian objects—hitching posts and mounting blocks—placed in a circular area before the main entrance. Although the sundial appears in this photograph to lie at one side of the central building, it is actually positioned at the exact center of a long allée bordered by oak and beech trees leading to the main road.

"The Captain's House" is all that remains of the original 17th-century plantation. This is one of two dependencies or subsidiary buildings which flanked a central structure, but which were not connected to it. The smaller building seen here may have provided space for the plantation's office or served, in part, as a place for the preparation of food.

For many generations life at Wye has been lived inside and out of a multitude of buildings. A store, a carpenter's shop, a blacksmith's forge, an ice house, a smokehouse, slave quarters, necessaries, a cow barn, a horse stable, a corn house, a sheep fold, and a greenhouse are known to have existed in the early 18th century. Added to this list in the 1780s were a dairy, loom house, wood house, and perhaps a marionette theater, each built off a service courtyard adjoining the new main house.

Wye's 17th-century boxwood pleasure garden—which survives in part in its overgrown 18th-century form—was 435 feet long and was probably made up of nine separate long rectangles containing flowers, grassy stretches, ornamental trees, and perhaps vegetables. Herbs were raised in another section of the grounds along with cutting flowers. The garden could be enjoyed from raised walks which crisscrossed the rectangles. There was also a raised terrace or mount at the far end of the garden, a pleasant area from which to view the grounds.

Left: *The service courtyard is a wide brick-paved expanse off the east side of the mansion, close to the kitchen wing and the wash or laundry room. The pediment of the dairy, seen at right, matches that of the main house. Also lining this handsomely designed space are a loom house, converted to a garage; a woodshed now used as a dog kennel; and a smokehouse, thought originally to have been a marionette theater.*

Below: *The front façade of the smokehouse repeats the same temple form found in the three main sections of the house and in the dairy. The inner arrangements of the building suggest that it was first used as a children's playhouse where marionette shows could be performed.*

The rear porch or piazza of the main house looks out upon a bowling green cut through the 17th-century boxwood garden in the 1780s or '90s. At the opposite end is the orangerie or greenhouse. Extending the entire width of the main section of the house, the porch was built in 1799 in pure Federal style with fluted columns and decorative capitals. The sides are fitted with wooden jalousies which provide both a screen of privacy and protection from strong crosswinds.

The addition of porches or piazzas to private homes was a late-Colonial development. It paralleled the gradual enlargement of the dwelling and the increased use of specialized space therein. The kitchen, for instance, was often located in a separate building, and the practice of using a summer kitchen divorced from the main house persisted through the 19th century. The three main sections of the 1784 Wye House —one of which included the kitchen— were built as separate units, and were linked together with "hyphens" or colonnades several years later; the Palladian portico at the front of the house was added at the same time. The rear porch was the last of the additions. It provides a unique vantage point from which to view the formal gardens, and affords a pleasant space for summertime entertainment, a leisure activity which a wealthy plantation family could indulge in the late 1700s. Only later in the Victorian period was the average American home provided with such an added space.

The orangerie took on its present form and name in the late 1700s, and is only one of several such totally separate buildings known to have existed in America at the time. The term reflects the upper classes' fascination with the raising of what were then exotic and sensitive fruits. The foundation of an even earlier building, simply called a greenhouse, is buried within the more elaborate structure. The high windows in the center section, facing south, allowed the fruit trees and ornamental plants stored within to receive a generous helping of sunlight during the cold months. A remarkably sophisticated hot air system fueled by a wood-burning furnace provided additional heat in the winter.

The orangerie lies at the foot of the formal boxwood garden and is here viewed from the porch of the main house. The bowling green was the principal area for gentlemanly games and garden parties from the 1780s on. Time has considerably softened the regularity and altered the scale of the broad avenue and its adjoining parterres.

At first glance the orangerie appears to be built of limestone blocks, but the material is brick covered with stucco and then rusticated. Vines have gradually covered over much of the façade, and there are no longer plants inside requiring light. Gone, too, is an 18th-century billiard table which was the centerpiece of a game room found on the second floor. Now at the Winterthur Museum, it is one of two such known American examples of the period.

A New Mexico Ranch

Outdoor living is virtually a way of life in the mountainous areas of the American Southwest where it is not only dry but reasonably cool a good part of the year. In the Rio Grande valley of north-central New Mexico one wants to be outside during much of the time, and traditional modes of building provide the space and ambience for graceful living. The courtyard or *placita* of this Pueblo / Spanish Revival ranch north of Albuquerque leads to nearly every room in the main house. Designed by John Gaw Meem and built in 1929 for Albert G. Simms and his wife Ruth Hannah McCormick Simms, the house incorporates an early Spanish Colonial ranch house.

Photographed in the winter, the outdoor scene is less colorful and joyous than in other seasons. But soon the fountain will be playing and the table set for dining or entertainment. In every season, however, the beautiful play of light and shadow can be seen along the portals and across the courtyard stones.

Left: *A great avenue formed by overarching trees leads from the entrance of the ranch to the main road. In contrast to the grounds of country homes in the East, the landscape is spare and seemingly unmanageable. Here, manicured lawns—unless constantly watered—are likely to blow away as dust. There is, however, a stark beauty in the clumps of flowering bushes and the isolated stands of pines seen against the western earth.*

Below: *The austere and simple entryway belies the warm and comfortable world to be found behind the massive oak doors. In times past when visitors were as likely to be unfriendly as friendly, the outside world was firmly closed off. A bell was there to summon those who were wanted within. Today, the portal provides much the same function as a front porch—a partially enclosed place in which to sit and enjoy a pleasant day.*

The simple beauty of the adobe residence is here perfectly realized. The slender posts and stripped beams or vigas *of the portal blend harmoniously with the smooth white walls, pedimented doorway, and flagstone paving. The feeling is of coolness and quiet —the kind of peace found in a true* outer *sanctum.*

The French Style in America

Located in the heart of the Louisiana river community of Natchitoches, the Ducournau building has been used as a residence and a store since the early 1800s. As in many areas of the South settled by the Spanish and the French, a great deal of attention has been given to exterior details. Space is devoted to the enjoyment of the outdoors on both the street front and behind the building. The widespread use of decorative cast iron for balcony railings, gates, columns, staircases, and complete porches or verandas in the 19th century contributes to the air of lightness and grace which so distinguishes these Southern buildings.

Right: *The Ducournau building overlooks the broad banks of the Red River. The splendid view can be enjoyed from the long balcony which can be reached from any one of six sets of French doors. As in the past, a shop occupies the first floor, and an apartment is situated on the second. Visible at left is one corner of the LaCoste building with its highly ornamental cast-iron veranda.*

Below: *A cast-iron staircase leads to the second-floor balcony at the rear of another building in the Ducournau-LaCoste row. Compact and imaginative in form, such winding stairs were often used in the 1800s as space savers. Today they are appreciated as much for their singular sculptural beauty and are particularly dramatic when used out-of-doors.*

The visitor to the Ducournau building reacts with special delight in discovering the inner brick-paved courtyard, reached through a carriageway from the street. The play of water from the fountain, the soft green plantings, and the tracery of iron fencing and sculpture combine to create a romantic and restful setting. The fence, rather than restricting, reinforces the same open feeling of space created by the widely separated posts and rails of the porch.

A Maryland Merchant's Elegant Town House

Chestertown, Maryland's River House is a more cooly elegant and conservatively designed home than its contemporaries found in rural areas of tidewater Maryland and Virginia. Built in the mid-1780s, the exterior of the town house is a classic study in sophisticated Georgian Colonial urban design; the interior incorporates traditional architectural detailing of the age of Chippendale. Thoughtful attention was given to the rear façade. The monumental two-story porch provides a splendid vantage point from which to view an almost endless procession of commercial and pleasure boats which make their way up and down the waterway of this historic port city.

Above: *The front façade of River House was probably always without the softening addition of shrubs or flower beds; foundation plantings would not have been in fashion in the late 18th century. A series of outbuildings was located across the narrow brick-paved street.*

Right: *The original two-story porch was removed in the early 1900s and replaced with a frame wing which projected out into the garden area. The Maryland Historical Trust, the present owners of the house, carefully reconstructed the porch in 1970 according to old photographs and evidence found on the site.*

Left: *The river garden is a cool, soft expanse of carefully tended lawn, flower beds, and boxwood. The walks are paved with old brick which harmonizes with the house and the vibrant reds of the roses and other flowering bushes. The view of the river is left unobstructed, and it can be enjoyed from a marble bench placed at the end of the center walk. Beyond and below the picket fence is a retaining wall which was built to prevent flooding of the grounds. In the distance may be seen the more spacious grounds of another Chestertown landmark, Widehall. A pergola is positioned near the end of the point; it is one of several such late 19th-century garden structures to be found on the property.*

Overleaf: *Full advantage is taken of the lower level of the porch during the heat of summer. Close to the basement kitchen, the covered walkway provides a pleasant dining area and a place for entertaining. The side garden is planted with hardy perennials and groundcovers which require little tending.*

Norwood House, A New York City Restoration

In any great urban center private space for outdoor living is very limited. Nowhere is this more true than in mixed commercial and residential areas. The Andrew Norwood House, dating from the 1840s, is situated in one such New York neighborhood, along once-fashionable West 14th Street in Manhattan. Only recently has the building been reclaimed for residential use; for much of the 20th century it served as a funeral home. The dedicated new owner has devoted most of his energy to the restoration of the interior, but the back yard has not been neglected. It has been cleared of years of debris and planted in a formal fashion that is in keeping with the severe neoclassical lines of the house and its interior architectural detailing.

Life away from the street can be peaceful if the surroundings suggest quiet and ease as they do here. The gray flagstone paving provides a unifying terrace base and repeats in tone the most decorative of the exterior architectural details, the weathered brownstone lintels and sills of the windows. Islands of greenery define an area for dining and entertaining. Flowering plants are placed in tubs so that they can be moved easily from spot to spot.

A formal parterre of miniature boxwood occupies almost half the Norwood House terrace. Usually not grown this far north, the bush can survive the cold and winds of winter in coastal areas of the Northeast if protected. The high brick walls effectively screen off the chill winds of winter and supply an attractive backdrop for the lush growth of ivy.

A Spacious Southern Cottage

The Tante Huppé House in Natchitoches, Louisiana, has little of the romantic glamor associated with the antebellum South. In many ways, however, it is more typical of the style of house built in a village or town by a well-established Southern family in the first half of the 19th century. The one-and-a-half story house, similar to cottage designs of the period, dates from 1827, and despite its seemingly small appearance, contains 18 rooms, 11 working fireplaces, and an unusual number of exterior doors—11 in all—each still with original locks and keys. The doors lead out to the full-length front veranda, to a long balcony or gallery at the rear of the second floor, and to a handsomely landscaped terrace at ground level.

This form of front porch, not attached but cut out from the main structure, is found in many 19th-century Southern and Border State homes, as well as in one-story bungalows which became popular throughout the country later in the century. Designs for cottages with this structural feature appeared in a number of building manuals or guides of the first half of the 19th century. The form is both functional and aesthetically appealing.

Summering by the Sea

For generations of North Americans, outdoor living has meant a summer vacation by the sea. In days when time seemed to move more slowly, it was even possible for some families to spend the whole summer at the shore, with father making at least weekend visits. Cape May on the southern New Jersey coast is a major American seaside resort town, and is, perhaps, its oldest. Visited from at least the late 1700s, the area reached a fashionable height in the second half of the 19th century. This is when a majority of its colorful Victorian cottages and villas were built, and at a time when New York and Philadelphia society preferred the Jersey coast to that of Maine, Nantucket, or Long Island.

Left: *The rows of Carpenter Gothic cottages form pleasant and imaginative patterns along Cape May's tree-lined avenues. Here, on the 600 block of Columbia Avenue, the inspired craftsmanship of the Victorian woodworker is well-displayed in the railings, brackets, latticework, and spandrels which make up the procession of front porches.*

Opposite page (top): *The Pink House (Eldridge Johnson House) is everyone's favorite Cape May dwelling. The fanciful woodwork of the two-story porch and the bargeboards decorating the eaves defy a straight line at every turn. The house celebrates in both its colors and ornamentation the exhilarating pleasures of summering by the sea.*

Opposite page (bottom): *The George Allen House is a much more sober dwelling, an Italianate-style mansion dating from the mid-19th century. Like other Cape May homes, however, it was obviously designed with consideration for outdoor living as well as more routine domestic needs. The great wrap-around veranda is an inviting feature; it provides an ideal place from which to enjoy the tastefully landscaped grounds.*

A Late-Victorian Residence

The Learnard House is located in Albuquerque's Huening Highland district, an urban neighborhood typical of the sort rescued from mindless neglect in recent years. Dating from 1897, the house was designed in an eclectic manner that defies stylistic definition. The wrap-around front porch is similar to those popular since the 1860s; the second-story sleeping porches (one for each of five bedrooms) were an addition of the 1920s. Porches for summertime sleeping gained great popularity in the early 20th century and were highly recommended by health experts, but were abandoned with the advent of air conditioning.

A swing or two was an important furnishing for a comfortable front porch. Other "moving" pieces like rocking chairs or platform rockers were also de rigueur *for the out-of-doors; the therapeutic effect of such motion was highly touted in the late 1800s.*

A Romantic 1920s Suburban Home

The Westhampton neighborhood of Richmond, Virginia, has been lovingly maintained since its establishment in the early 1900s by many of the city's professional and merchant class. The homes are spacious and solidly built; extensive landscaping provides a welcome screen of privacy from the flow of city traffic, and behind these walls of greenery are inviting expanses of lawn and garden. Many of the homes are neoclassical or Tudor Revival in style, and the gardens are less rigid and confining than those of either the Colonial or Victorian periods. On the grounds of the 1920s home illustrated here there has been a studied attempt to evoke a continental European atmosphere; the garden room, added in 1967 along with the terrace, was intended to give the effect of an Italian loggia that had been enclosed with glass. The addition of terra-cotta sculptural figures and containers strengthens the romantic feeling sought for the setting.

The main entrance of the house is nearly submerged in a stand of lofty pines. The usual American sweep of lawn is found behind the house where it can be enjoyed in privacy. There is no attempt made to make a public display of house and garden from the road. As in many Latin countries, the picturesque is displayed from within and not without.

A quiet, secluded bower was formed under the branches of a great oak. This is a perfect place for a stone bench and an Italian terra-cotta figure which has lost its moorings but not its charm.

The terrace and garden room are found behind the house, on a level below that of the first floor. Designed by Richmond architect Thomas A. Gresham, the area faces east, thereby taking full advantage of morning sun and afternoon shade. The terrace has generous space for dining and entertaining and is paved with Pennsylvania flagstone. Flowering plants are arranged in planters and pots which can be moved indoors when the weather is inclement.

Right: *The garden room serves also as a music room and library. It is a place where the family can enjoy various leisurely pursuits and is considerably more imaginative in function and form than today's typically dull "family room" for TV viewing and relaxation. The Buckingham slate floor is covered with grass mats.*

Below: *The interrelatedness of the indoor and outdoor spaces is emphasized by the garden room's five graceful archways, three of which serve as windows; French doors at each end of the row open up into the terrace.*

4.
In the Garden

Few aspects of an historic property are more appealing to the eye and the senses than a well-tended garden. To stroll through the carefully composed grounds of the Governor's Palace at Williamsburg or to wander along the romantically winding paths of Middleton Place's azalea gardens near Charleston is to experience the full flavor of an artfully designed landscape. A prominent place for flowers, shrubs, and trees is essential for almost all period residences—whether or not the historical record dictates the present horticultural scheme or not. It is perfectly reasonable, however, to assume that at some time in the past the ground upon which an old house was built was laid out with some thought in mind as to its visual appeal. Just what *was* there at any given time and what *is* appropriate today are two prime concerns. The answers are difficult for even an archaeologist to supply, but the search may be as pleasurable as a promenade through an old pleasure garden.

The forms of nature are ever-changing. What was planted 100 or 200 years ago may have disappeared completely or have reached an overgrown state barely resembling that known in the past. Judicious pruning and careful replanting of old species are often the only requirements for returning the grounds of a house to a semblance of their original condition. In other cases, new specimens will have to be substituted for the old. Lists of the varieties of plants grown in the past are not difficult to come by; considerable imagination, however, must be devoted to duplicating or approximating them. While scientists have been able to improve the hardiness and form of many species, they have not always been able to preserve particular specimens.

The kind of plants grown in a particular location may have been determined by availability and climatic conditions. As historian James Marston Fitch has explained, landscape materials "are even more the prisoners of specific environmental parameters than are architectural ones." From Thomas Jefferson's garden journal and other papers one learns, for instance, that boxwood—then obligatory on the grounds of so many Virginia plantations of the period—was not planted at Monticello. Presumably, it would not flourish in the cooler mountain-top setting. Such equally fashionable, but hardier, plantings as rosebay rhododendron, lilac, English yew, trumpet vine, and English ivy, however, were found at Monticello. There were also a number of exotic varieties which Jefferson had imported from England or bought from Philadelphia horticulturist Bernard McMahon, and these were unlikely to have been planted on other properties.

The search for appropriate plants for a particular setting can go on and on. What thrived 100 years ago may not do as well today. On the other hand, with improved species, what was a failure in the past may be a blooming success today. Plants popular in the early 1800s such as sweet William, pinks, balsam, primroses, and bluebells were not as widely used in the 1880s. The zinnia, for instance, was not introduced until the 1860s, but rapidly gained favor as a bedding plant. For detailed and extremely useful advice on recreating period landscape settings, the reader is advised to consult the lists of "authentic" plants for four major periods of American gardening compiled by Rudy J. Favretti and Joy Putman Favretti in *Landscapes and Gardens for Historic Buildings.* This is also a useful source for the names of nurseries and seed houses that offer old varieties.

The ways in which gardens were laid out in the past are a great deal easier to discover than what was planted in them. It has long been known that Colonial gardens were arranged in a formal, symmetrical manner. Beds and walks were laid out in as straight

Governor Jonathan Belcher Place, Milton, Massachusetts; house built in 1776, grounds laid out in 1781. Four equal squares planted with flowers and roses constitute the formal garden as it existed in 1936. Some aspect of this space was probably once devoted to vegetables as well. Note that the central walk is positioned in a direct line from the main house and, at the opposite end, leads to a terrace and a summerhouse.

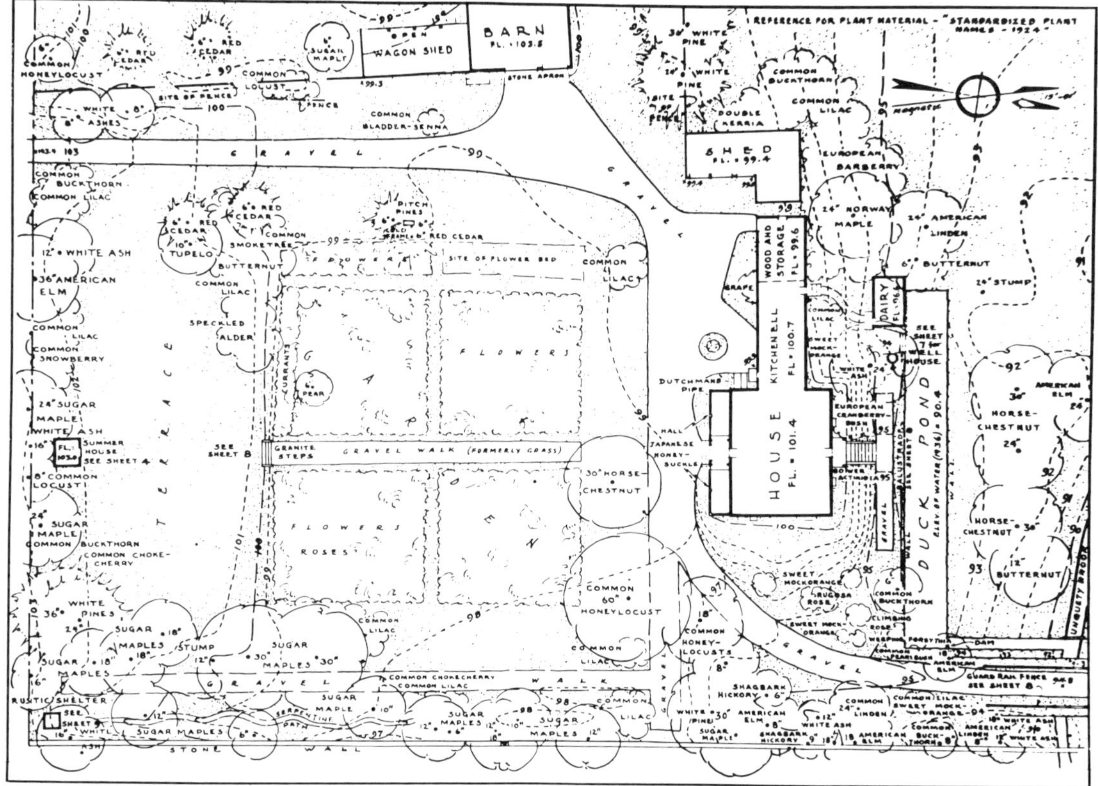

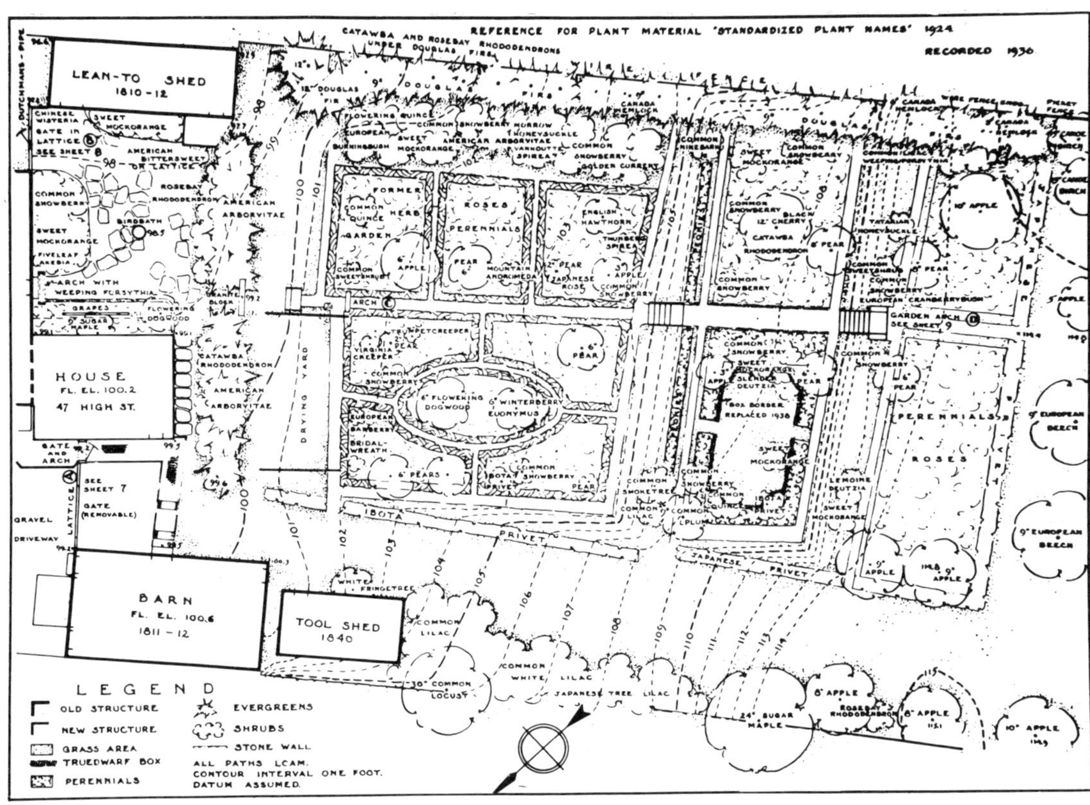

Pierce-Knapp-Perry Place, Newburyport, Massachusetts; house built 1811-12; garden laid out c. 1815. The grounds of this Federal-period home depart somewhat from the strict geometric plan favored in the previous century. For topographical and climatic reasons, gardens in the North were often not laid out in a straight axis from the mansion house. This garden is built on a gently sloping site and has been terraced in three levels.

an axis from the house as possible. This is clearly evident at Wye House on Maryland's Eastern Shore (pp. 40-45) and at the Governor Jonathan Belcher Place, Milton, Massachusetts, illustrated on p. 66. Another version of this basic scheme can also be seen in a recently constructed 18th-century garden located in suburban Philadelphia (pp. 37-39). As with other aspects of Colonial culture, the formal arrangement was a natural borrowing from English tradition, a practice proscribed by limitations of space. Space, of course, was more plentiful in the New World, but the inclination to follow strict geometric form persisted well into the 19th century, especially in the South. Symmetrical gardens were in almost every sense formal outdoor living areas designed to provide well-defined walks for promenades and quiet places for reading and conversation. Nearly all such formal arrangements were enclosed by wooden fences or walls of stone or brick. These were designed to keep out wandering animals and to preserve a sense of privacy.

Despite their appeal to the modern imagination, English pleasure gardens were, nonetheless, rare in the colonies. The art of landscaping was one that could only be indulged by the very wealthy; the formal gardens planted by the royal governors, in fact, were those most successful in their imitation of Old World custom. These gentle-

Stone alleyway looking east toward Union Street, Nantucket, Massachusetts. Vertical wood fences or paling was most often used to enclose gardens and lots; sometimes, as at left, it was combined with a stone foundation. "The facility and quickness with which they are put up," one architect wrote in 1856 of picket fences "[and] their cheapness and showiness are their strong recommendations."

men were able to import rare plant materials as well as the decorative objects—statuary, sundials, urns and vases—which often give a garden an air of dignity and ease. The average 18th-century residence was unlikely to have been surrounded by a profusion of decorative plants and shrubs, and what formal garden area that existed was often devoted to the growing of more useful vegetables and herbs. As late as 1834, J. C. Loudon, an English horticulturist, commented about the American scene: "Landscape gardening is practiced in the United States on a comparatively limited scale; because in a country where all men have equal rights, and where every man, however humble, has a house and garden of his own, it is not likely that there should be many large parks [pleasure gardens]."

George Washington, who possessed more than the equal rights of common men, was one of the economically privileged class to possess a "large park." In addition to the famous colonnaded portico added to the river side of Mount Vernon and the raising of the mansion's roof line, the pleasure grounds (or what was also termed at the time "the family living area") were enlarged after the Revolution. Two formal gardens, planted in the 1760s in a strict rectangular fashion, were reshaped in a more curving, naturalistic form; the beds and walks within, however, remained basically symmetrical. A courtyard had been formed by the addition of curving and covered walkways leading to a series of dependencies at each side of the main house. Beyond the courtyard began the bowling green or lawn, bordered by serpentine avenues which came together at the far end of the lawn at a ha-ha wall or fosse separating the park from the

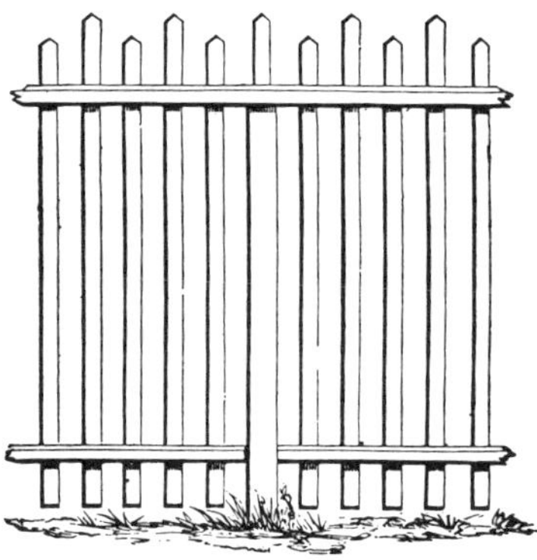

Picket fence design from Village and Farm Cottages *(1856). Improvements in fencing materials and new designs were frequently suggested during the 19th century. This model was recommended for the separation of lots, and featured extra-thick palings enclosed between double rails. "Train along such a fence the Wistaria vine," the authors recommended, "and in the season of bloom you will have a lovely wall of verdure, surmounted by a glorious cornice."*

meadows. The overall plan was an advanced one for America at that time and represented a decided break from the formal style of garden design toward a more natural one. The informal treatment was further advanced at Jefferson's Monticello and at "The Vale" (plan illustrated on p. 8).

Jefferson began planning the grounds of his mountain-top home in the late 1700s, but it was not until his retirement in 1809 that he was able to devote considerable time to his ambitious schemes. Progressive in every respect, he fully subscribed to the naturalistic school of landscape design popular in England during the second half of the 18th century, and he depended on Bernard McMahon, a Philadelphia horticul-

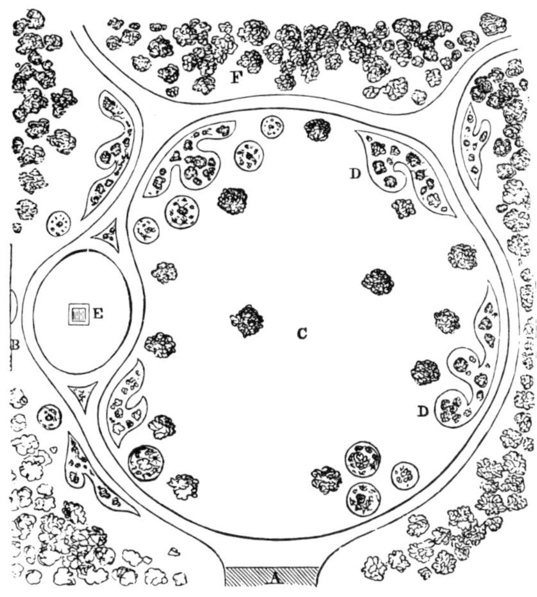

The "Natural style" in gardening was urged upon the home owner in the mid-19th century by professional landscape architects. This design is from the 1856 Illustrated Annual Register of Rural Affairs, *where the essence of romantic landscaping was explained: "The flower beds and shrubbery should . . . be sufficient to conceal such portions of the walk as are remote from the spectator, who should see only that portion immediately before him. The continued curve to the right or left as he advances, affords a constantly varying scence and a pleasing succession of views."*

Cottage design from Village and Farm Cottages. *The typical working-class home in a small town or rural setting was rarely as neat as this engraving suggests. The sparseness of the plantings and the absence of any foundation shrubs, however, is an accurate rendering. Behind the dwelling is a well house.*

turist and author of *The American Gardener's Calendar* (1806), for plants and advice. Rather than breaking up the grounds into precise geometric shapes, Jefferson preferred great open spaces with low plantings which mixed shrubs and perennials; instead of straight paths radiating from the mansion, there was a curving gravel walk before the front, and a rambling "roundabout" encircling the lawn at the back. The picturesque was emphasized at every turn, and, while the natural line was favored, Jefferson was not at all reluctant about giving nature a helping hand. His notes regarding a wooded area of the grounds ("The Grounds in General"), penned in 1771, testify to his love of romantic effects:

> Thin the trees. Cut out stumps and undergrowth. Remove old trees and other rubbish except where they may look well. Cover the whole with grass. Intersperse Jasamine, honeysuckle, sweet briar, even hardy flowers which may not require attention. Keep it in deer, rabbits, Peacocks, Guinea poultry, pidgeons &c. Let it be an asylum for hares, squirrels, pheasants, partridges and every other wild animal (except those of prey.) Court them to it by laying food for them in proper

Above: *Vhay House, Santa Barbara, California, 1825. It is probable that plantings around the veranda of this early adobe homestead were nearly always luxurious. The training of flowering shrubs in this manner was highly recommended for all climates.*

Below: *Plan for a rosarium from* Beautifying Country Homes *by Jacob Weidenmann (1870). The plan allowed for the display of seventeen varieties, and made use of pyramidal frames of wire or wood. The beds were to be cut out of the lawn.*

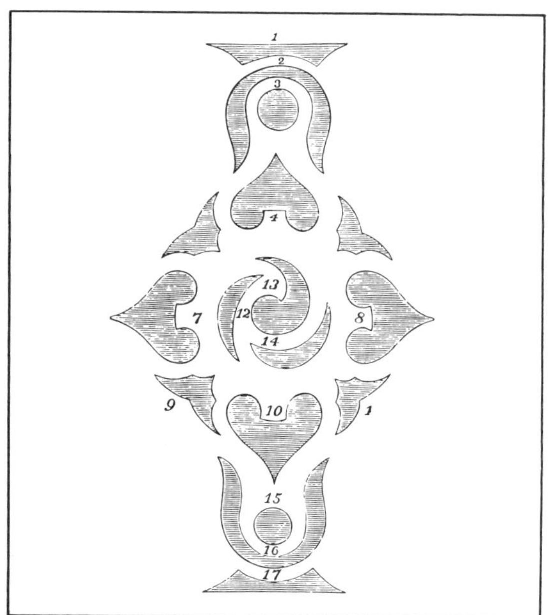

places. Procure a buck-elk to be as it were Monarch of the wood; but keep him shy, that his appearance may not lose its effect by too much familiarity. A buffalo might perhaps be confined also. Inscriptions in various places, on the bark of trees or metal plates, suited to the character or expression of the particular spot. Benches or seats of rock or turf passim.

There is not evidence to suggest that Jefferson was successful in attracting such a wide variety of wildlife, but his practice of mixing flowers and shrubs in informal groupings along winding paths and as occasional borders was widely applauded and imitated for years after Monticello began to fall to ruin and the grounds to revert to nature. Landscape architect A. J. Downing, and his disciple Calvert Vaux, further developed the theories of Jefferson and McMahon in the 1840s and '50s. Until at least the Civil War, considerable attention was paid to producing softening and subtle effects through the use of climbing vines; mixing different species and sizes of shrubs in gentle clusters; introducing such decorative ornaments as classical vases and formations of rocks; and positioning such ornamental trees as the weeping willow and the Lombardy poplar at picturesque vantage points. The formal regularity of the Colonial garden was now considered impossibly stilted and unnatural.

Above: *"Natural and picturesque rock-work," from the* Illustrated Annual Register *(1873). The author warned against the formal arrangement of rocks into "artificial" conical piles; rather, rocks were to be placed "on the side of a slope, bank, or side of a ravine—just at those places where in nature, beds of rock are to protrude." One purpose of a Victorian garden was obviously to imitate nature.*

Right: *A handsomely terraced and enclosed Victorian suburban lot from* The Art of Beautifying Suburban Home Grounds *(1870) by Frank J. Scott. "That kind of fence is best," Scott advised, "which is least seen, and best seen through."*

In the last quarter of the 19th century the art of landscaping finally achieved a popular level of acceptance and practice. This was also a period when there was a gradual turning away from naturalistic compositions and a return to the more regimented and regular. The mid- to late-Victorian home was often built on a high foundation, and plantings to hide the monumental base became a requirement. Flower beds, previously formed along curving paths, were now introduced into the lawn area as "carpet bedding." The varieties available for show—coleus, canna, and other variegated plants—were more luxuriant and larger in size; colors were more intense, and double-flowered varieties were favored over the single. A plethora of cast-iron and rustic wooden objects—described more fully in the final chapter of this book—began to dot the domestic landscape. Rose gardens were very much in vogue, a number of varieties often arranged in complex geometric parterres.

The introduction of the lawn mower in the 1860s was to transform the common domestic scene. A writer in the 1886 *Register of Rural Affairs* reported that lawn

A mower made by R. H. Allen & Co., New York, and recommended in the Illustrated Annual Register *(1886). "It cuts a strip a foot or more wide, as fast as a man will walk. . . ."*

mowers "have been greatly improved . . . so as to obviate the necessity of using the lawn scythe; and they have another great advantage, namely, little or no skill or practice is required to use them while making a perfect and even green carpet." So began America's love affair with the uniformly trimmed lawn, an area that the experts advised in the 1880s be cut at least every two weeks rather than only several times a season. By the turn of the century, lawns had become greatly enlarged and carpet beds and other obstructions were being removed, leaving behind, in some instances, only foundation plantings and a scattering of trees and shrubs at the edges of the greensward. For the average American household, the lawn, and not the garden, was now the center of outdoor living.

The wealthy of the late Victorian period could well afford to devote attention to a picturesque garden as well as a luxurious lawn. Old-fashioned formal rose gardens in the Colonial manner were among the popular approaches to beautifying the grounds of the new and old rich alike. By the early years of the 20th century, more efficient earth-moving equipment allowed land to be shaped into highly imaginative forms—rock gardens, oriental tea gardens, and terraced spaces in the Italian sytle with reflecting pools and stone sculpture. A professional resident gardener was usually on hand to keep such specialized formal landscaping in near-perfect condition. Many of the estates of America's aristocrats rivaled those of even England's most venerable families.

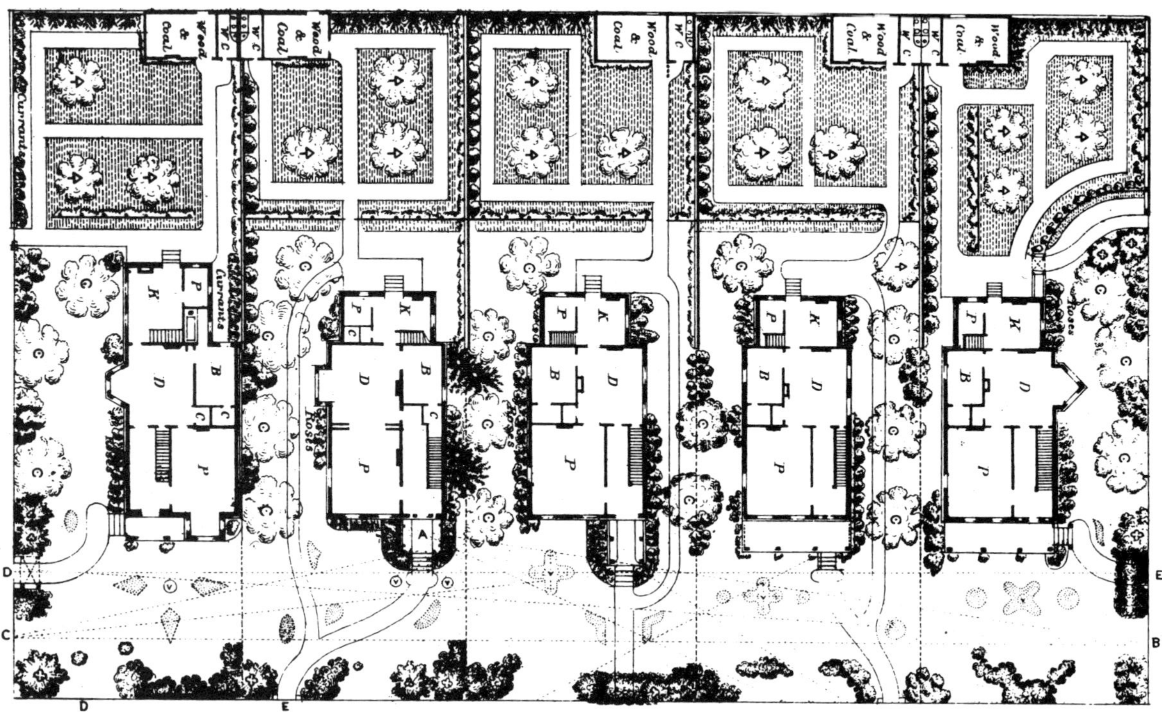

A model suburban block as designed by Scott. Although the lots are strictly rectangular, considerable care is given to providing as much diversity of space as possible. Note the use of regular foundation plantings, then coming into vogue.

North side and garden, Ransom E. Olds House, Lansing, Michigan, late 19th-century. The meticulously manicured and gracefully composed grounds of this home reflect an appreciation of the social value of an inviting setting. The terrace and pool area provide relief from what is basically a flat and uninteresting site. The low cast-iron fence does not intrude upon the scene, but rather ornaments it.

In periods of rapid economic change—either boom or depression—the fragile natural environment created by careful husbandry is likely to suffer. During the Depression years, for example, it was impossible for many families to maintain the expansive gardens laid out in more prosperous times. Since World War II, the steady march of inflation and the rise in land values have made extensive landscape gardening a luxury affordable only by the very wealthy. It is much easier and cheaper to maintain most of one's property in grass; some would even substitute Astroturf. Economic and space limitations, however, need not dictate a paucity of aesthetic response. As is clearly evident from the much smaller private properties of Europe and the Far East, tradition need not be swept aside for convenience. There is a workable level of adaptation for the owner of a period property, an approach that is historically representative in the type of plantings used and in the way in which they are arranged.

5. Outdoor Structures: Summer and Garden Houses

Of all outdoor living spaces none possess more charm than the garden house and the summerhouse, the latter building also known in the 19th century as a gazebo, pavilion, or arbor. Although these free-standing structures serve some practical purpose—providing shelter from the sun and rain as well as useful storage space—their main reason for existing has been the visual delight they convey to the domestic landscape. Such buildings rarely survive today on the grounds of the average old house, but they often still occupy a prominent position on more ambitiously landscaped properties. Equally picturesque, but more modest in form and practical in use, are such other decorative accents as the pergola, rose arbor, arched gateway, and the well enclosure or well house. Even the simple country cottage property of the mid-19th century was likely to include one or another of these features.

The North American practice of embellishing lawn and garden areas with outbuildings and protective or supporting structures had its origin in the 17th and 18th-century pleasure gardens of England and the Continent. While many of the forms originated in yet earlier times—the pergola, for instance, derives from classical Italy—it was not until the rise of landscape architecture as an art in the 1600s that so much attention was devoted to beautifying the grounds of a private residence with specialized buildings. Although there was little time available to pursue the English landscaping schemes in Colonial America, there were men of private wealth or political position, however, who could afford to indulge aristocratic follies. The Wye House orangerie/greenhouse, with a billiard room on the second floor (pp. 44-45), is one such example. The Charles Carroll home, Mount

Cottage design from Village and Farm Cottages *(1856) by Henry W. Cleaveland, William Backus, and Samuel D. Backus. The grounds of this inexpensive country cottage (cost in 1856, $1,100) are by no means elaborate, but include a picturesque well house in the style of a summerhouse. "Let no such cottage stand in a bleak, open field," the authors wrote, "as if it had been accidentally dropped there, and forgotten."*

Clare, in Baltimore, is known to have had a similar building in the 1760s, as did the John Tayloe plantation, Mount Airy, in tidewater Virginia.

The Wye formal garden also included a garden house situated in a prominent position at the end of a long boxwood allée. This one-room building served as a formal resting place from which to view the garden. The fashionable style in the 18th century

Village house design from Village and Farm Cottages. *An elegant residence required more elaborate surroundings, in this case a rose-covered arch and what appears to be a cast-iron summerhouse. Among the plantings are such favorites as rose of Sharon and hollyhocks.*

was Georgian, and a garden house might incorporate pilasters, an ornate cornice, round arch sash, and other classical elements. A garden house on the Colonel Isaac Royall estate in Medford, Massachusetts, dating from the mid-1700s, was built in an octagonal form with a cupola and a finial figure topping the shingled roof.

After the Revolution America's expanding merchant and patrician class devoted more and more time to the elaboration of the grounds of their country estates. Elias Hasket Derby was a particularly ambitious Massachusetts merchant who commissioned Samuel McIntire to design three garden houses, one of which survives in Danvers, having been moved from the family farm in Peabody. This neoclassical garden house is a remarkable building and was situated in the center of a formal garden noted for its exotic plantings. Even more exceptional, however, is another of Derby's buildings which disappeared from view during the 19th century. This was a rustic hermitage built in a bower at the end of the central garden path. English pleasure grounds of the 17th and 18th centuries are known to have featured such an ornamental dwelling, a romantic "ruin" which served no other purpose than that of lending an air of romance and mystery to the grounds; a suitably bedraggled "hermit" was usually hired to lurk about the premises. Derby, perhaps at a loss for a liv-

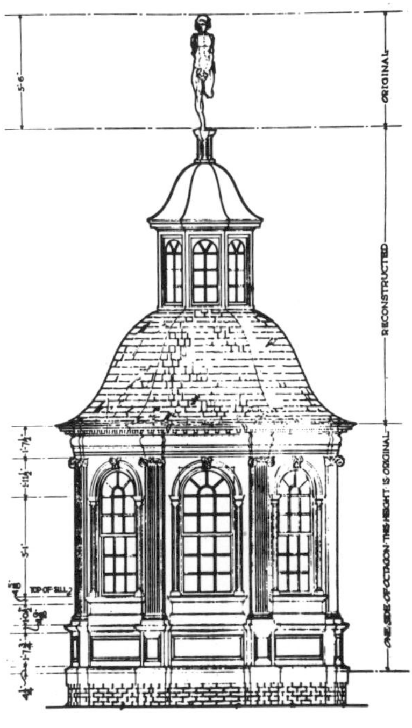

Garden house, Colonel Isaac Royall House, Medford, Massachusetts, mid-18th century. The octagonal shape was a favorite one for garden structures and derives from European designs for pavilions.

ing derelict, had a wooden figure of a hermit carved for him in 1793 and placed in the hut. According to an observer in 1802, the effect was convincing:

> The hermitage . . . was scarcely perceptible at a distance; a large weeping willow swept the roof with its branches and bespoke the melancholy inhabitant. We caught a view of the little hut as we advanced thro' the opening of the trees; it was covered with bark; a small low door, slightly latched, immediately opened at our touch; a venerable old man was seated in the center with a prayer book in one hand while the other supported his cheek, and rested on an old table which, like the hermit, seemed moulding to decay . . . a tattered coverlet was spread over a bed of straw . . . I left him impressed with veneration and fear which the mystery of his situation seemed to create. . . .

Garden house, originally located at the Elias Hasket Derby farm, Peabody (South Danvers), Massachusetts, 1793-94. The building, wrote one observer in 1802, has a "fine airy appearance and commands a view of the whole garden." The arched entrance was originally open and matched an arched opening on the other side of the building.

Except for 20th-century lawn grottoes built of whitewashed truck tires, it is unlikely that anything quite as bizarre has been attempted in North American gardens since that time.

Love of classical forms for garden structures persisted well into the 19th century, this despite the growing taste for an informal, natural style of landscaping. The first garden house built at "The Vale" in Waltham, Massachusetts, in 1793 was a small square Roman temple open on three sides. It was erected against the garden wall at the meeting point of several paths winding through the informally laid-out grounds. Circular temples or pavilions, open to the elements, were also in vogue during the first half of the 19th century, especially in the South where Greek Revival architecture enjoyed considerable popularity.

The typical garden house was situated in an area devoted to fairly formal arrangements of flowers and shrubs; in contrast, a summerhouse might be located some distance away from the main house and the flower garden. At "The Vale" the octagonal summerhouse, built in the early 1830s after

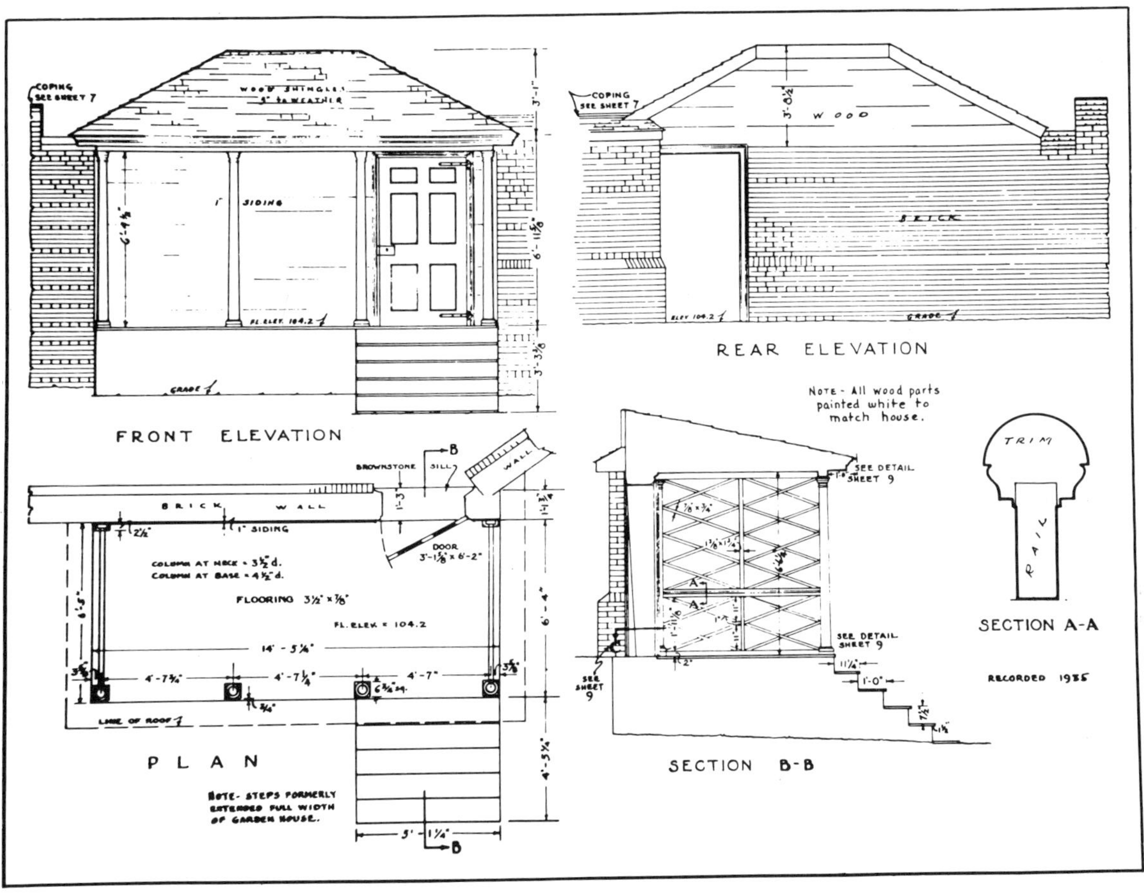

Garden house, "The Vale," Waltham, Massachusetts, 1793. The drawing shows the steps as they existed in 1935; they originally stretched the width of the building. The door leads to higher wooded ground beyond the brick garden wall.

the garden house, is found in a high, semi-wooded area overlooking the property. Its style is greatly different from that of the garden building, the columns being twisted in the Venetian manner and the windows cut out in a segmental fashion. The feeling is a much more informal one, as if this were a private place for relaxation rather than a setting for proper social engagements.

During the 19th century the architecture of outdoor buildings gradually shifted away from the classical to the rustic and the fanciful. Structures built of peeled logs and tree trunks, and ornamented with branches, were considered by landscape architects of the time more "natural" and fitting for the American scene. "They admit a great display of taste and ingenuity, with but little cost," one writer proclaimed in 1873, "an important consideration where the motto of the people must be 'profuse of genius, not profuse with gold.'" Inexpensive and imaginative, rustic work was also popularly embraced for outdoor furniture and ornaments such as vases and urns. The other material which was introduced for outdoor use in the mid-1800s was cast iron. Its graceful, airy quality and the relative ease of assembly of prefabricated forms made it a

Left: *Pavilion, Gainswood (General Nathan B. Whitfield House), Demopolis, Alabama, 1842-60. Garden houses were sometimes termed pavilions, and on this extraordinary Greek Revival estate there were two such structures built as circular temples. A wicker rocker is faintly visible in this fragment of an old photograph.*

Below: *Garden house, Cortland, New York, 1828. Moved to its present location in 1935, the building was originally located on the grounds of the W. R. Randall home. Only the center door of this Greek Revival outbuilding is real; the same arrangement of two false and one real door is repeated on each of the other sides. It is said that Mrs. Randall, the wife of the town's leading merchant, often entertained friends to tea in the 15' x 15' garden house.*

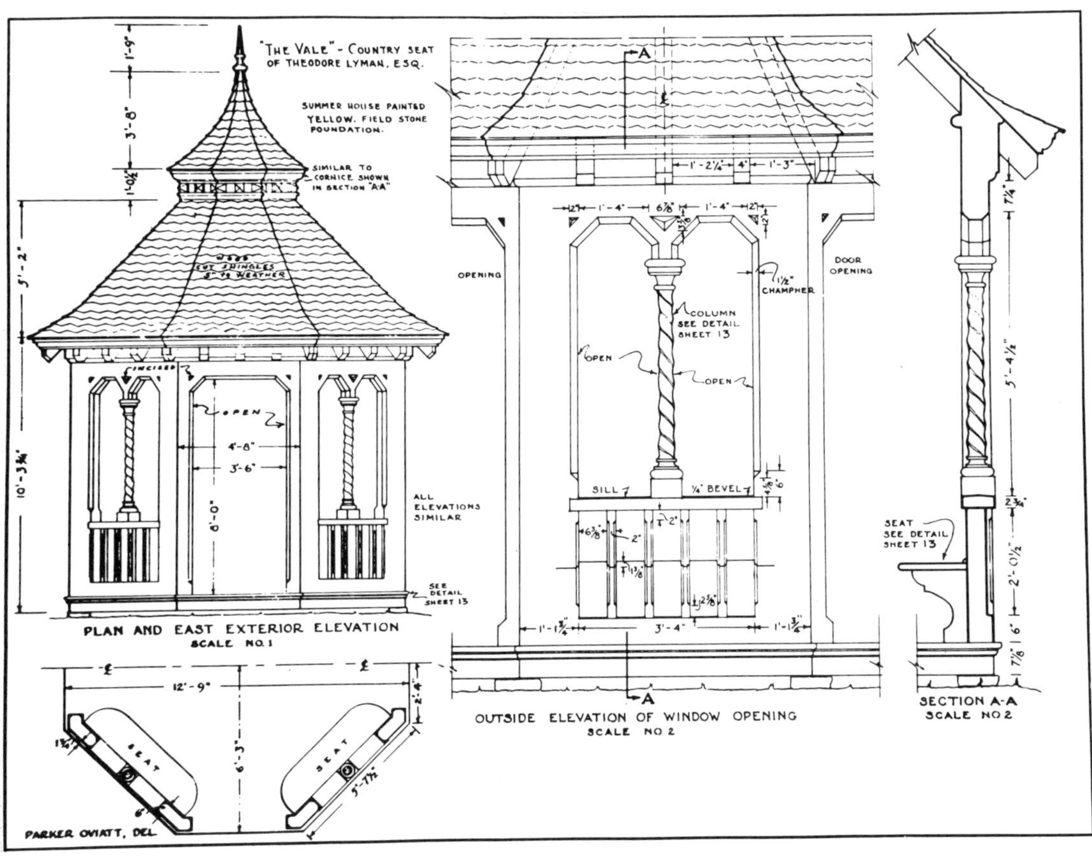

Summer house, "The Vale," Waltham, Massachusetts, prior to 1833. Once again, the octagonal from was favored, but the decorative treatment is radically different from that employed in the estate's earlier garden house illustrated on p. 77.

favorite for summerhouses.

Outdoor architecture became more and more imaginative in its forms as the 19th century progressed. The garden house disappeared and the summerhouse grew more elaborate. A particularly ornamental summerhouse was sometimes termed a gazebo. Laced with gingerbread and latticework, it was, in effect, a fanciful playhouse. At a time when most people still "vacationed" at home or, if they were city dwellers, on the farm and in rural villages, a recreational abode perched on a grassy mound or cantilevered over the edge of a pond was a highly desirable feature. But because this type of building was often casually built and even more haphazardly maintained, a majority of them no longer survive.

The return to simpler styles of domestic architecture in the early 1900s, to the Georgian Colonial and to Beaux Arts classicism, brought with it a corresponding change in the appearance of outdoor living areas. They became formalized, more constricted. Highly ornamental summerhouses were out of place. Terraced spaces were defined by clipped hedges and were entered through curved lattice archways; grape

Left: *Design for a prospect tower from the* Illustrated Annual Register of Rural Affairs *(1873). A desire to rise above ground level to observe one's eminent domain is reflected in this design. The rustic tower, according to the architect, could be placed "on any wooded hill where an extensive view is afforded."*

Below: *Rustic shelter, Governor Jonathan Belcher Place, Milton, Massachusetts, early to mid-19th century. Such an informal building was not located in the garden, but was, rather, hidden away on the grounds.*

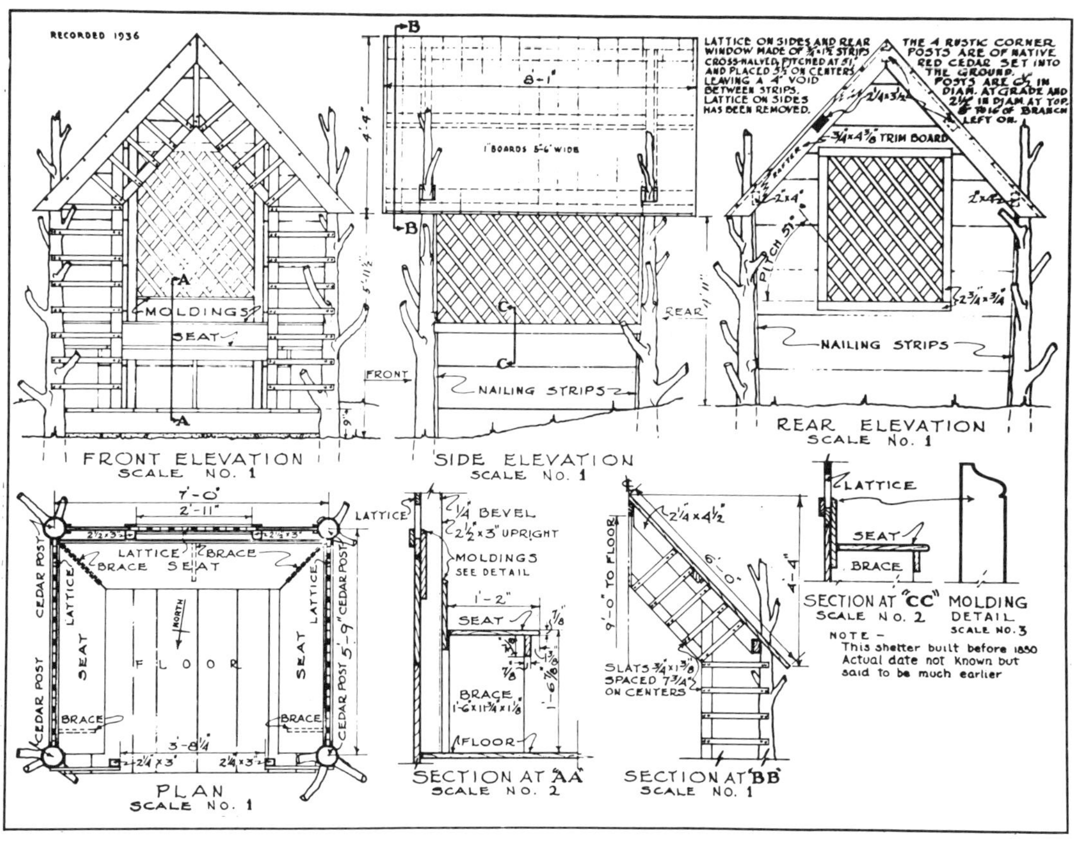

vines, roses, and wistaria were trained to the straightforward lines of a pergola. There was a retreat from the separate summerhouse back to a screened porch or piazza of the main house and its adjoining formal yard and garden. Some of the most beautiful and ambitious private gardens were created during this period, designs based on Italian and French models of elegant composition, but these were often frozen in marble, or at worst, concrete. This was the suburban way —carefully contained, easily maintained spaces which were pleasant to look at but without character or imaginative content.

There are many old properties today which would be enhanced by the addition of a garden- or summerhouse, regardless of whether such a building existed in the past. The loss of such outdoor structures has not been compensated for by the awning-covered terrace or the poolside cabana. Plans for various models of this old-fashioned type of shelter are scattered throughout this chapter to illustrate the many design possibilities. Usually simply built, they not only provide an interesting decorative accent to the grounds, but a practical and graceful retreat from the noise and demands of modern living.

Above and below: *Two rustic arbor designs from the* Illustrated Annual Register of Rural Affairs *(1873). Cheapness of construction was one of the principal arguments for rustic work. The roofs of such arbors were thatched of straw, and the remaining building materials could be gathered easily in the woods.*

Above (left): *Rustic pump house design from* Barns, Outbuildings, and Fences *(1870) by George E. Harney. Few were the outdoor appurtenances on a farm or in a rural village which were not interpreted and dressed up in the rustic style during the second half of the 19th century. The style was also considered appropriate for urban parks, including New York's Central Park.*

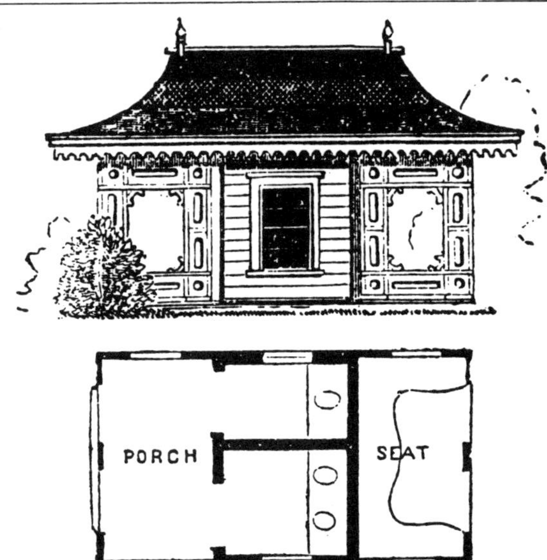

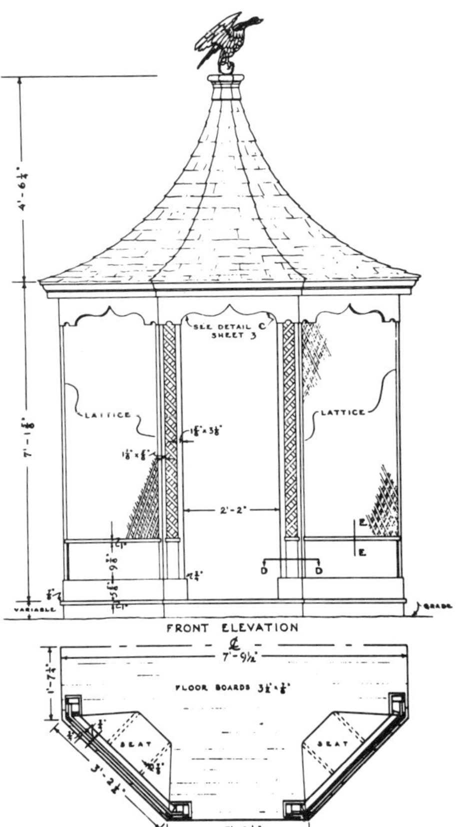

Above (left): *Design for a composite wrought- and cast-iron summerhouse from the New York Wire Railing Company catalogue (1857). "Airy summer-houses, dotting verdant lawns," the manufacturer wrote, "are spots so attractive that a rural residence, well-appointed, is sure to have them. . . ." He chose to illustrate the most popular of forms, the octagonal, but noted that others — "square or round, plain or elaborate" — were also available.*

Above (right): *Design for a garden outbuilding from* Villas and Cottages *(1857) by Calvert Vaux. This quite ingenious design combined the basic facilities of the outdoor privy with those of the summer or garden house, much like the modern swimming pool cabana.*

Left: *Summerhouse, John Cabot Place, Beverly, Massachusetts, early 19th century. The octagonal shape remained popular throughout the 1800s, but the decoration of the shelters evolved from the very simple to the complex. The current vogue for romantic Gothic forms is suggested in the ogee arches of the fascia.*

Opposite page. Above (left): *Summerhouse, Ashhurst estate, Mount Holly, New Jersey, early 19th century. The Chinese fretwork panels, used in place of the usual latticework, and the pagoda form suggest that this building was designed to be used as a tea house.*

Opposite page. Above (right): *Swiss summerhouse design from* Detail, Cottage and Constructive Architecture *(1873) by A. J. Bicknell & Co. Picturesque "Swiss" cottage designs had been popular in America since A. J. Downing introduced them in the 1840s. Gradually — in the hands of others — these buildings acquired more and more gingerbread.*

Opposite page. Below: *Summerhouse, Boulder Farm, Hopkinton, New Hampshire, mid-19th century. What better place for a summer retreat than high up on the very boulder which gave the property its name? This hexagonal building is reached by means of a ramp.*

C
C
A
D
D
F
F
B
E
E

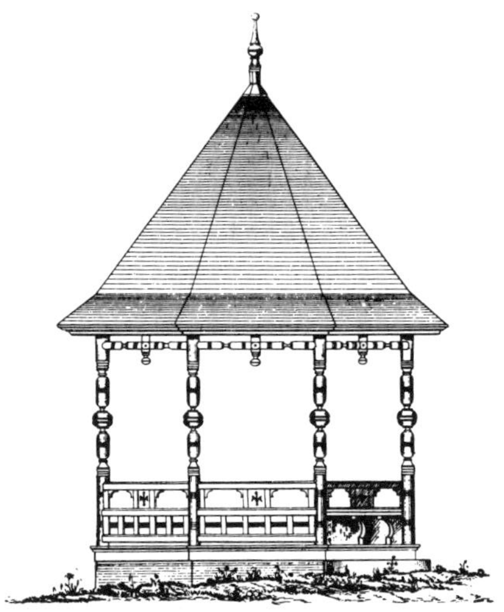

Above: *Designs for summerhouses from* Modern Architectural Designs and Details *(1881) by William T. Comstock. The design at left is a familiar octagonal one; the second, at right, a Queen Anne model, is imaginatively positioned on a rocky slope.*

Left: *Summerhouse, Wisconsin Club (Old Milwaukee Club), Milwaukee, Wisconsin, late 19th century. This extraordinary building stands as a perfect architectural expression of high Victorian romanticism. Every angle of the summerhouse was designed and decorated to delight the eye, to outdo nature in inventiveness of form.*

Opposite page. Above (left): *Design for a grape arbor from* Woodward's Architecture and Rural Art *(1867) by George E. Woodward. The Italian pergola was first introduced to North America in the mid-1800s in the angular form illustrated here. Later pergolas were more rigidly classical in design.*

Opposite page. Above (right): *Rustic pavilion, Wethersfield, Connecticut, late 19th century. Built on a promontory overlooking a cove, this building combined rustic work and gingerbread. Airy, graceful, and picturesque, it epitomizes the best in eclectic Victorian architecture.*

Opposite page. Below: *Most of the outdoor structures built during the 19th century for fun and fancy are now in ruins or have been swept away for kindling. This latticework garden house was photographed in the 1930s somewhere in Alabama, forgotten and forlorn.*

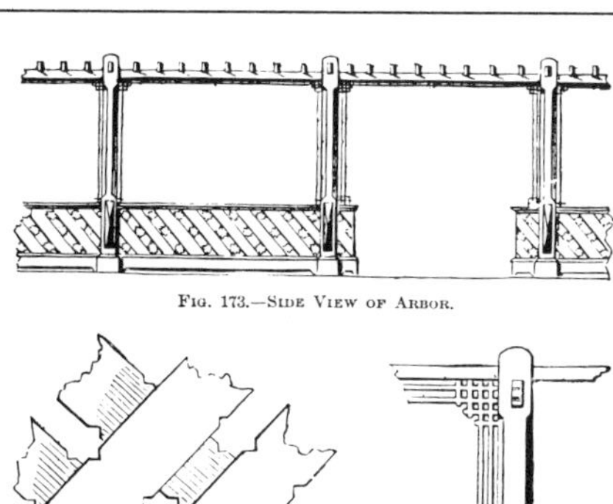

Fig. 173.—Side View of Arbor.

Fig. 174.—Detail of Arbor. 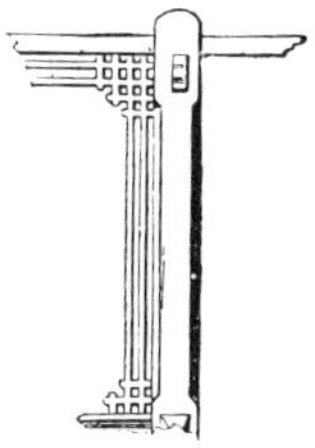 Fig. 175.—Detail of Arbor.

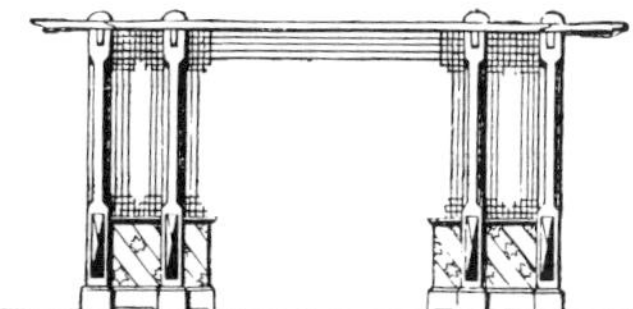

Fig 176.—Cross Section.

6.
Outdoor Furnishings

The furnishings of porch, terrace, lawn, and garden areas have changed over time from the simple to the complex to the simple again. During the Colonial period, when the average house had few structural or horticultural features of note, there was not much to furnish. By the early 19th century, however, when porches and porticos, flowers, gardens, and well-defined lawns were the middle-class norm, interest in suitable furnishings—from fountains to lawn and porch furniture to sculpture—increased dramatically. After the Civil War, in fact, a number of landscape architects warned that the passion for outdoor "decorating" had gotten completely out of hand. "Avoid spotting your lawn with garish carpentry," one wrote in 1870, "or plaster or marble images of any kind, or those lilliputian caricatures on Nature and Art called rock-work." The advice went unheeded for many years, but the appeals for restraint were to prevail in tasteful circles by the early 1900s.

The imitation of nature was an urge which was foreign to the early settlers; they were much too busy attempting to tame the land. Those fortunate enough to possess sufficient income to support the development of English-style pleasure grounds had to import decorative items from Europe. The sundial was one such object, and it often assumed a place of importance in the center of a formal garden (see p. 37) or in a forecourt (see p. 40). Furniture was restricted mainly to the homemade variety—benches or settles which were positioned in a shady nook. By our standards, the grounds of even the most stately 18th-century home would have appeared cold and uninviting at the time.

As outdoor spaces were enlarged and improved during the 19th century, it followed that they be furnished more ambitiously. At first the decoration was minimal and in keeping with the prevailing neoclassical taste—urns or vases of stone, composition, or wood for the lawn and garden, simple

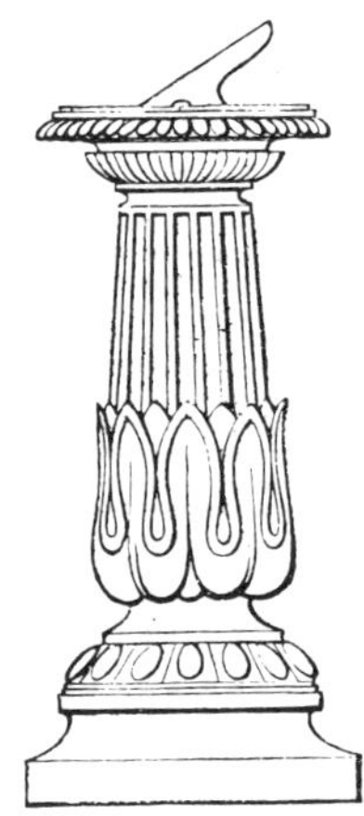

Design for a sundial from Woodward's Architecture and Rural Art *(1867) by George E. Woodward. A simple Ionic column often served as the shaft of a Colonial-period sundial; in the mid-19th century, this had been elaborated with acanthus leaves and other motifs.*

Cast-iron vase from the New York Wire Railing Co. catalogue (1857). Priced from $5 to $20, these objects were used as planters.

benches of stone or wood. More romantic and picturesque notions were emphasized in furniture made of twigs, branches, and roots. Rustic work of the type used for arbors and summerhouses was thought most appropriate for porch and lawn furniture—in particular chairs, settees, tables, and stools. With raw materials right at hand, there was no end of possibilities for the home craftsman. Vases of rustic design became immensely popular for plantings. Durability, however, was frequently sadly lacking. One critic warned in 1870 that "any constructions of this kind which suggest flimsy wood, or bungling carpentry, or rotting bark, or want of firmness at the base, though they may give a pretty effect at first, soon became rickety nuisances."

The fashion for outdoor furniture which imitated the forms of nature was to persist well into the 20th century, but form and

Above: *Rustic stool and chair from* The Illustrated Annual Register of Rural Affairs *(1873). The back and seat of the chair illustrate a common feature of rustic work—wood mosaic. A variegated appearance is achieved by using rods or sticks of different colored bark in vertical and horizontal patterns.*

Below: *Summerhouse table and "garden-sofa" from* Barns, Outbuildings, and Fences *(1870) by George E. Harney. Objects such as these usually lasted a few seasons and then reverted to nature, but they could be duplicated quite easily.*

Ladies' veranda rocker and lawn chair from Montgomery Ward & Co.'s catalogue (1895). The back and seat of the rocker were made of reed; the posts of a durable hardwood. The chair combined soft- and hardwoods in a fanciful yet sturdy manner.

construction improved considerably with the use of more sophisticated materials such as bamboo, reed, rattan, and cast iron. Stylish rockers for the veranda or porch became standard items. Lawn and porch swings or gliders provided a pleasant, amusing diversion for children and adults. Whole sets of outdoor furniture—four chairs, a table, and a settee—could be purchased ready-made from furniture dealers and through mail-order catalogues. Canvas and denim were introduced in camp stools

Lawn swing from the Sears, Roebuck and Co. catalogue (1908). Termed "the best swing on the market," this model was designed to seat four "passengers" comfortably. Such an entertaining apparatus was common on picnic and camp grounds of the late Victorian period and was a special treat on the home scene.

and deck chairs, pieces of a desirable light weight that could be stored more easily than the primitive solid-wood rustic contrivances used earlier in the century or the later cast-iron furniture.

No material proved more durable outdoors, or more receptive to artistic treatment, than cast iron. Economical in price and manufactured in numerous locations from the mid-1800s on, cast-iron furniture was designed as much to delight the eye as to provide comfort. Iron was cast in a great variety of patterns which imaginatively captured the fanciful forms of nature. The one objection to the material—then as now—was its hardness. Calvert Vaux recommended in 1857 that porches should be provided with "permanent or movable seats, but these should be of wood in preference to iron, as the latter is a very cold, unyielding, and unsatisfactory material for such a purpose." He had no objection to the use of cast iron on the lawn—in the form of statuary, vases and urns, or fountains. Animal figures—dogs, deer, and lions—were especially popular at the time, and not until later in the century, when some lawns resembled the grounds of a zoo, were there calls to limit the cast-iron animal population.

Today such cast-iron sculpture is prized for its "folk art" qualities, and, if still positioned on a lawn, must be bolted down to a cement base to be secure from theft. Unfortunately, no one seems to want to steal plaster burros pulling carts, pink flamingoes, or miniature wooden windmills. These geegaws of the first half of the 20th century have not aged sufficiently to attract anything more than passing interest. Similarly neglected is the popular porch and lawn furniture of the period, of which the metal chair with a shell-shaped back and the sway-back canvas deck chair are two notable examples. Mass produced, they possess little

Cast-iron grape settee and chair, and morning-glory chair, from the New York Wire Railing Co. catalogue (1857). Relaxation was not encouraged in these convoluted pieces of seating furniture. Only by sitting bolt upright could one avoid indentations in the back. Visually, however, they could not be improved upon.

Right (above): *Folding porch or deck chair from the Sears, Roebuck & Co. catalogue (1902). Nothing more comfortable for outdoor use has been invented, but sturdiness has not been a strong point. Most models have ended up junked as soon as the frame slipped from its grooves.*

Right: *Cast-iron greyhound and lion from the New York Wire Railing Co. catalogue. Creatures such as these found a comfortable resting place on the lawn or at the sides of an entryway. They were usually sold in pairs. The greyhound or whippet was Prince Albert's favorite canine and was first copied as sculpture in America by the Janes, Kirtland Co. of Philadelphia in 1850.*

Below: *Entrance to Woodruff Place, Indianapolis, Indiana, lithograph by Braden and Burford, c. 1888. Laid out in 1872, the subdivision was enjoying its fashionable heyday when this rendering was made. All the cast-iron ornamental scultpure and ornaments were manufactured by the J. L. Mott & Co. ironworks in New York City.*

ENTRANCE TO WOODRUFF PLACE.
INDIANAPOLIS, IND.

Above: *Fountain and pool, Woodruff Place.*

Right: *Large urn on pedestal, Woodruff Place. The present light fixtures date from the turn of the century; they replaced gas fixtures.*

Right (below): *Fountain and pool with standing figure of Liberty, Woodruff Place.*

of the artistic appeal of many of the earlier outdoor pieces. They are simply items of convenience, useful for a season or two in the sun and then often thrown away.

The past was a less wasteful period. When making improvements to the grounds of a house, the average 19th-century American was seeking some sense of permanence, of lasting beauty to be enjoyed by future generations. Whether the property was a small lot or a larger expanse, an effort was made to imitate nature—even to outdo her. The same attitude which guided the improvement of "home grounds," led to the establishment of great urban public parks as well as to the creation of private neighborhood enclaves such as Woodruff Place in Indianapolis (illustrated here in a series of photographs) and New York City's Gramercy Park. While the impulse to embellish every aspect of a natural setting sometimes led to public and private excesses, these extremes were simply amusing exaggerations of the prevailing taste. Neither the cast-iron deer nor the exuberantly ornamented summerhouse were intended to serve an insistent practical need; they were small pleasures of delight, and sometimes of rare beauty. No old house requires a fanciful veranda or a graceful portico to make it a home, but such additions, carefully made, can add to a property's character and its real value. To be able to recapture some aspect of this heritage from the past can be an immensely satisfying adventure.

Illustration Credits

In this list of illustration credits, sources not specifically identified in the captions are given. The following abbreviations are used to denote position on page: a *(above),* b *(below),* m *(middle),* t *(top),* l *(left), and* r *(right). Illustrations from the archives of the Historic American Buildings Survey (National Architectural and Engineering Record) are identified as HABS.*

Cover/jacket: Michael Kanouff (a-l, a-r, and b-l); Allison Abraham (b-r).

P. 1, *The Art of Beautifying Suburban Home Grounds* by Frank J. Scott (1870); pp. 2-3, HABS; p. 5, Scott.

Introduction: p. 6, HABS, p. 7, Scott (a) and HABS (b); p. 10, HABS; p. 11, HABS; p. 12, HABS (a-l) and (a-r) and Library of Congress (l).

Chapter 1. p. 13, *The Art of Beautifying Suburban Home Grounds* by Frank J. Scott (1870); p. 14, HABS; p. 15, HABS (a and b); p. 16, HABS, (l and b); p. 17, HABS (a-l, a-r, m, and a); p. 19, HABS (b-l and b-r); p. 20, HABS (a and b); p. 21, HABS (b and r); p. 23, HABS; p. 24, HABS.

Chapter 2. p. 25, Library of Congress; p. 26, HABS (l and b); p. 27, HABS; p. 28, HABS; p. 29, HABS; p. 30, HABS; p. 31, HABS.

Chapter 3. p. 33-37, J. Michael Kanouff; p. 38, Charles Gale & Son (t) and J. Michael Kanouff (b); pp. 39-45, J. Michael Kanouff; pp. 44-45, HABS (t); pp. 46-48, Allison Abraham; pp. 49-57, J. Michael Kanouff; pp. 58-59, HABS, Jack E. Boucher; p. 60, Allison Abraham; pp. 61-64, J. Michael Kanouff.

Chapter 4. p. 65, *The Art of Beautifying Suburban Home Grounds* by Frank J. Scott (1870); p. 66, HABS; p. 67, HABS; p. 68, HABS (t); p. 70, HABS (a); p. 73, HABS.

Chapter 5. p. 74, *The Art of Beautifying Suburban Home Grounds* by Frank J. Scott (1870); p. 75, HABS (b); p. 76, HABS; p. 77, HABS; p. 78, HABS (l and b); p. 79, HABS; p. 80, HABS (b); p. 82, HABS (l); p. 83, HABS (a-l and b); p. 84, HABS (l); p. 85, *Beautifying Country Homes* by Jacob Weidenmann (1870) (a-r) and HABS (b).

Chapter 6. p. 86, *Beautifying Country Homes* by Jacob Weidenmann (1870); p. 89, HABS (b); p. 90, HABS.

Selected Bibliography

Only those publications currently in print or readily available from public libraries are included in this listing. Many of the basic source books on American horticulture and landscaping have not been reprinted and remain inaccessible to the general reader.

Betts, Edwin M. and Hazlehurst Bolton Perkins, *Thomas Jefferson's Flower Garden at Monticello.* 2nd edition. Charlottesville, Va.: University Press of Virginia, 1971.

Bicknell, A. J. & Co. *Detail, Cottage and Constructive Architecture.* Reprinted in *Victorian Architecture.* Watkins Glen, N.Y.: American Life Foundation, 1978.

Clifford, Derek. *A History of Garden Design.* New York: Frederick Praeger, 1963.

Comstock, William T. *Modern Architectural Designs and Details.* Reprinted in *Victorian Architecture.* Watkins Glen, N.Y.: American Life Foundation, 1978.

Favretti, Rudy J. *Early New England Gardens, 1620-1840.* Sturbridge, Mass.: Old Sturbridge Village, 1962.

______ and Joy Putman Favretti. *Landscapes and Gardens for Historic Buildings.* Nashville, Tenn.: American Association for State and Local History, 1978.

Fisher, Robert B. "Following Washington Down the Garden Path." Reprinted from *Landscape Architecture* (May, 1976). Washington, D.C.: National Trust for Historic Preservation, 1978.

______. *The Mount Vernon Gardens.* Mount Vernon, Va.: The Mount Vernon Ladies' Association, 1960.

Fitch, James Marston. "Preservation Requires Tact, Modesty and Honesty Among Designers." Reprinted from *Landscape Architecture* (May, 1976). Washington, D.C.: National Trust for Historic Preservation, 1978.

Leighton, Ann. *American Gardens in the Eighteenth Century.* Boston: Houghton Mifflin, 1976.

______. *Early American Gardens.* Boston: Houghton Mifflin, 1970.

Lichten, Frances. *Decorative Art of Victoria's Era.* New York: Charles Scribner's Sons, 1950.

Lockwood, Alice G. *Gardens of Colony and State.* 2 vols. New York: Charles Scribner's Sons, 1931.

Noel Hume, Audrey. *Archaeology and the Colonial Gardener.* Williamburg, Va.: Colonial Williamsburg Foundation, 1974.

______. "Historical Archaeology in Garden Restoration." Reprinted from *Landscape Architecture* (May, 1976). Washington, D.C.: National Trust for Historic Preservation, 1978.

Scott, Frank J. *The Art of Beautifying Suburban Home Grounds.* Reprinted as *Victorian Gardens.* Watkins Glen, N.Y.: American Life Foundation, 1979.

Taylor, Raymond L. *Plants of Colonial Days.* Williamsburg, Va.: Colonial Williamsburg Foundation, 1968.

Van Ravenswaay, Charles. *A Nineteenth-Century Garden.* New York: Universe Books, 1977.

Vaux, Calvert. *Villas and Cottages.* Reprint of 2nd edition. New York: Dover Books, 1970.

Weidenmann, Jacob. *Beautifying Country Homes.* Reprinted as *Victorian Landscape Gardening.* Watkins Glen, N.Y.: American Life Foundation, 1978.

Woodward, George Everston. *Woodward's Victorian Architecture and Rural Art.* Watkins Glen, N.Y.: American Life Foundation, 1978.

Wright, Richardson. *The Story of Gardening.* New York: Dodd, Mead & Company, 1934.

Index

Since the terms "Colonial" and "Victorian" are far too broad to be anything but generally descriptive, they do not appear in this index. Consult the breakdown of the larger periods into component parts (i.e., Georgian, Gothic Revival, Italianate) under Architectural styles.